DEEP TIMES WITH GOD

DEVELOPING AN INTIMATE WALK WITH GOD REQUIRES
DISCIPLINE, PATIENCE, AND TRUST

DR. CHARLES MAKOUNDI
Author - Academic - Researcher

Ark House Press
arkhousepress.com

© 2023 DR. CHARLES MAKOUNDI

All rights reserved. Apart from any fair dealing for the purpose of study, research, criticism, or review, as permitted under the Copyright Act, no part may be reproduced by any process without written permission.

Cataloguing in Publication Data:
Title: Deep Times with God
ISBN: 978-0-6459673-4-0 (pbk)
Subjects: REL012040 [RELIGION / Christian Living / Inspirational]; REL012120 [RELIGION / Christian Living / Spiritual Growth]; REL023000 [RELIGION / Christian Ministry / Discipleship];

Design by initiateagency.com

Contents

Book summary v
Dedication vii
Foreword ix

Chapter One: The Existence of God 1
Chapter Two: Challenges are Part of Everyday Life 19
Chapter Three: God Still Does Miracles 46
Chapter Four: Resilience and Pursuit 64
Chapter Five: Divine Protection 72
Chapter Six: Divine Guidance 86
Chapter Seven: The Finish Line 121

References 129
Endorsement 1 131
Endorsement 2 132
Endorsement 3 135
Endorsement 4 137
Endorsement 5 139

About the Author 141

Book summary

This book is a compilation of my spiritual encounters while walking with God. It clarifies how I felt about God's goodness, faithfulness, love, protection, and holiness throughout my life. In the face of life's uncertainty, the reader's journey through the book could offer psychological support and solace. Regardless of the reader's life challenges, this book gives hope that God is still up to something to change someone's life. Although overwhelming, discouragement may have caused a sense of despair. A child of God will never lose hope until God has spoken the final word. This book teaches students who lack the resources to keep up with their studies that nothing is insurmountable. Those who feel they have tried everything and have reached a dead end could find comfort in this book. We can still have hope if we are alive. Being interested in what other people have experienced in life, to avoid repeating their mistakes or, at the absolute least, to strengthen our own relationship with God, is in my opinion for our own good as God's children.

Dedication

All the glory goes to God for his guidance and insights in writing this book. The Holy Spirit has been my source of inspiration and my best friend ever since I had an encounter with God. Thank you, my Lord Jesus Christ, for dying on the cross for me and saving me from the power of sin.

This book is dedicated to my family members and in-laws, who have always been there in moments of mourning, dancing, darkness, and light.

Hats off to my lovely wife, "My Honey," Michelle Claire Scholastique Makoundi, for living together and always being by my side. You are a co-visionary and co-dreamer in the same boat as me!

Our daughter Melissa Emmanuelle Makoundi is a gem in our family. I profoundly admire your sense of humour when you often say, "Dad, you are again on your computer—please take some rest."

To my late father Joseph Makoundi, my late mother Malemo Moline, my late uncles Pierre Bissouekémé and Gaston Nzihou, and my late sister Josephine Makoundi.

To my late brother Noel Nzihou and late sister Melanie Nzihou. To my late father-in-law Michel Nkembo, my late mother-in-law Cecile Nkembo, and my late sister-in-law

Bertille Nkembo. I wish you had been here to witness this book launch.

Finally, a person who had shared his journey with me was the late Rev. Kirk Idika Joseph, my spiritual son, who left us unexpectedly. Kirk, your spiritual legacy will not be forgotten. I believe you are in heaven, and we shall meet there.

I always keep the above-mentioned souls in my heart until we meet again.

Foreword

Praise the Lord! "DEEP TIMES WITH GOD" is an interesting book to read and experience how to become closer to God. Jesus says in Luke 5: 4 "Launch out into the deep".

This book will assist you if you wish to comprehend something deeply in your walk with God. This book has seven chapters. Seven represents the fullness of God's work. Your connection to God will be strong.

What a privilege to write a foreword note! Rev. Dr. Charles Makoundi has a very close relationship with God. You'll comprehend what I'm saying once you've finished reading this book.

I highly recommend this book to everyone, not only to read but to practice.

I believe that when you read, you will have a deep understanding of the Word of God and a close relationship with God.

My prayer is that those who read this book will be blessed.

By the grace of God, Rev. Dr. Charles Makoundi will write more books and glorify the Kingdom of God.

God bless you.

Rev. Dr. Philip Jayabalan
President of GLOBAL MISSION INTERNATIONAL
and Pastor of VICTORIOUS LIVING
ASSEMBLY MALAYSIA

CHAPTER ONE
THE EXISTENCE OF GOD

This book encapsulates the deep times I have been with God. It is a lengthy recap of my precious times under the guidance of the Holy Spirit when I felt vulnerable, being tossed up and down by the vicissitudes of life. The book also records the stupid things I did, and the lessons learned while walking with God. We are told that Enoch walked with God which always makes me think about my own journey with God up until now.

Genesis 5:24

"Enoch walked with God, and he was not, for God took him."

In this book, the readers join me on a journey to find out the many spiritual lived experiences that have shaped my life. Choosing to walk with God should be a life commitment. There are a lot of opinions about the existence of God. Many books have been published about the origin of God, but none has fully put into words with convincing arguments the nature of God and His attributes other than the Bible. The Bible has given us the most simplistic yet profound explanation of who God is.

The origin of God finds its roots in where we have all failed to explain how this whole universe came to be. In Genesis 1: 1-5 (e.g., Amplified Bible), the Bible explains succinctly how God created the Earth and Heaven.

Genesis 1: 1-5

Verse 1 says "in the beginning God created [by forming from nothing] the heavens and the earth. Verse 2. "The earth was formless and void or a waste and emptiness, and darkness was upon the face of the deep [primeval ocean that covered the unformed earth]. The Bible says God is spirit.

The Spirit of God was moving (hovering, brooding) over the face of the waters. Verse 3. And God said, "Let there be light"; and there was light. Verse 4. God saw that the light was good (pleasing, useful) and He affirmed and sustained it; and God separated the light [distinguishing it] from the darkness. Verse 5. And God called the light day, and the darkness He called night. And there was evening and there was morning, one day.

From this biblical passage, I note that God is spirit which means He is non-material. We cannot portray God in a human form. He formed the galaxy ex nihilo [latin "out of nothing"]. What is interesting is that God can hear us when we pray. He can feel the pain we go through. He directs our steps when

Chapter One: The Existence of God

we count on him for guidance. In this book, the reader learns more about the characteristics of God. The Bible also says that there was only one spirit that was hovering upon the waters from the beginning which makes me believe that there is only ONE GOD but not many Gods as other thinkers, philosophers, and scientists have argued.

Geologists have been trying to explain how Planet Earth came to be. They also came up with an approximate age of 4.54 billion years for Planet Earth, which most scientists seem to agree with. The age of the earth is an estimate with an uncertainty of 0.05 billion years (Jain, 2014). Mathematically, 0.05 billion years is 50 million years, and represents a margin of error. Despite many advances in geochronology which is dating geological rocks through time, the age of the earth is an estimate.

This simply means we cannot come up with an accurate age of the Earth. This ongoing effort to know about the formation of the Earth has been tainted with inaccuracies thus implying how limited mankind is when it comes to the pursuit of knowledge. I have a Doctorate degree (PhD) in Geoscience, but I always marvel at the fascinating picture of creation.

Charles Darwin (1809–1882), an English naturalist, geologist, and biologist, was widely known for his contribution to evolutionary biology. He proposed that all species of life derive from a common ancestor. However, he failed to include God in his theory and ignored the existence of the creator of that ancestor. With over 25 years of academic experience in the earth sciences, I think science without God loses its essence. God must be put in the equation to explain in the best possible terms some of the most complex scientific questions science has never answered.

As an academic and researcher in geoscience, I believe God has given mankind the ability to think and innovate to some extent by being aware that we are still limited in our understanding of the universe. The constant or unending desire to discover the undiscovered makes us avid to know more and more about the universe compared to the unlimited God, the one who knows everything-he does not need to be taught or lectured on any subject.

As a geologist, I still wonder about the source of the mineral zircon, which is used to date geological rocks. There is some explanation for the bonding of ions to form chemical molecules, thus bringing into existence mineral species such as zircon. The origin of life cannot be explained by the human brain. Everything began with God. Period!

Was the Earth a nebula before it began to form? Thousands of questions remain unanswered-that's where I think we are constantly striving to reach the unknown. God is a deity, and a deity is a divine being.

Personally, God has appeared to me in dreams, sometimes in the form of an angel or a magnificent bright light. One day, I had the opportunity to see the oval throne of God in a vision. It was a very spacious, bright, and glittering domain surrounded by many rooms. I couldn't count the rooms because there were far too many, in my opinion. And I heard a voice telling me that the shadows that you see in each room are angels working day and night to serve God. Each one of them has a role to play. They can be sent to Earth to accomplish a mission. Then I came back to my senses-that was a vision. It reminds me of Jacob who saw in a vision, angels ascending and descending on a stairway that linked Earth to Heaven. As it reads in the passage below.

Chapter One: The Existence of God

Genesis 28:12

"He had a dream in which he saw a stairway resting on the earth, with its top reaching to heaven, and the angels of God were ascending and descending on it."

The Oxford Dictionary defines a "deity" as a supernatural being who is considered divine or sacred. I came to know of God's existence by revelation well before my conversion to Christianity. I knew there was something wrong in my relationship with the "infinite dimension—the infinite being who is God." I found myself floating, or existing like a "float," without any connection to the source where I came from.

This book is a collection of my spiritual experiences as a result of what I went through in my home country and abroad. It unpacks my reflection on the goodness and faithfulness of God in my life. The reader's journey through the book may provide psychological support and comfort in the face of life's uncertainties.The readers will find a number of facts that could potentially serve as spiritual tools to improve their relationship with God.

Jeremiah 29:11

"I know the plans that I have for you, says the Lord, plans for peace and not for woe, to give you a future and hope."

Life may seem difficult, but God guarantees us a bright future. This book is for those who have lost hope and are left to fend for themselves. The Lord is changing the parameters that control your life. Those parameters may be disease, the loss of loved ones, the loss of a job, etc. God's power can transform your life in the face of all adversity. To students who do not have the financial means to cope with their studies, this book tells you that nothing is impossible. This book could provide comfort to those who think they have reached the end of the road and nothing has worked for them. As long as we live, there is still hope.

Today, you may be a modern-day Job, as documented in the Bible. According to the Bible, Job was prosperous until one day he lost everything (Job 1: 13-22). Remember Job in the Bible? He got back twice what he had lost. I believe there is a double portion coming your way at some point in the name of Jesus, our Lord and Saviour.

This book echoes God's promises as the main source of provision and peace. The Bible says in Psalm 23:1: "The Lord is my shepherd; I will not lack for anything." A shepherd takes care of his flock and protects it from all dangers. A shepherd treats his sheep fairly. He ensures that his sheep have the well-being they deserve. God gives each of us what we want according to our level of faith.

Hebrews 11:6

> *"But without faith, it is impossible to please God; for he who comes near to God must believe that God exists, and that he is the rewarder of those who seek him."*

Chapter One: The Existence of God

I have experienced firsthand the awesomeness of God. This book is for those who may have lost their faith, become lukewarm, or are experiencing a decline in their intimacy with God. My prayer is that after reading this book, the reader will be able to re-ignite their passion for the things of God's Kingdom, that they will be able to bounce back and regain momentum, leading to the fulfilment of their destinies in God. The landscape of this book is a composite picture of the oracles of God in my life. When my biological parents could no longer finance my education, my Heavenly Father (God) took over and made a way where there seemed to be no way. The Bible says in Jeremiah 33:3: "Call on me, and I will answer you; I'll tell you great things, hidden things you don't know."

God therefore wants us to know him so that we can benefit from all the blessings that are ours. The Bible says in John 10:10, "The thief only comes to steal, slaughter, and destroy; I have come so that the sheep may have life and have it in abundance."

I do not know what Satan has stolen from you, but God can give you back what you have lost. If Satan has destroyed your marriage, know that it is not too late; God will restore your life. Remember the story of Job, who lost almost everything but received a double portion of what he had lost at some point in his life? What an incredible God we have by our side every day, everywhere, and every time.

This book is also intended for people who are in business but have not made progress and have become discouraged. They may be on the brink of giving up. Discouragement may have overwhelmingly triggered a sense of despair, but for a child of God, there is always hope until God has said his last word.

Haggai 2:9

> *"The glory of this last house will be greater than that of the first house, says The Lord of Hosts; and it is in this place that I will give peace, says The Lord of Hosts."* God has already stored a series of miracles distributed in time and space, the catalyst of which is faith in God.

My mother had waited ten years for me to come into existence. She tried with all the means available to her so that I could be born. But her efforts were in vain, and she had given up hope. Ten years later, she became pregnant when she least expected it. Coming into this world, I grew up in dire conditions as my father was no longer working. He took an early retirement because of his precarious state of health. In fact, my father worked for the national railway company of Congo (CFCO) as a train driver and mechanical engineer. Dad loved his work and even received an award in mechanical engineering. As much as I can remember, my dad began to lose his sight in 1977.

In my culture, a spell can be cast over someone. The spell comes in the form of sickness or bad luck. Later, my dad was bewitched by his own older biological brother—a long story to put in words in this book. Consequently, Dad became partially blind and had a limited amount of mobility due to impaired sight. I think I should inform the readers here that casting a spell over a person is also known as witchcraft. People who practice "black magic" or witchcraft aim to use occult forces to harm other people for selfish purposes. This practice has been deeply rooted for generations in the sub-Saharan African region (Kohnert, 1996).

It is also known that witchcraft is associated with early deaths, the inability of a wife to conceive, failure in school examinations, and several other areas where witchcraft limits what a person can achieve (Bongmba, 2007). I have spoken with many friends in Australia who have briefly shared their experiences with me about witchcraft. Nyabwari and Kagema (2014) argued that personal experience and knowledge about witchcraft are realities for many Africans. The authors further explain that mystical power is often experienced by many Africans who have grown up in Africa. They may have witnessed magic, divination, witchcraft, or other mystical phenomena.

In my childhood, I had a sweet and sour experience. A sweet childhood was based on how I enjoyed my dad's company every day. On the contrary, I had a sour childhood upbringing because of the difficulties I had navigating various situations with Dad and Mum. I remember Mum travelling to the city of Brazzaville to file Dad's retirement application. My sister and I were left with Dad alone for about three months. It was hard to be with Dad and look after him daily, yet I had a sense of someone whose joy never ran dry. According to the Bible, the joy of the Lord is my strength (Nehemiah 8: 10). In every moment of my life, I always ask God to fill me with His joy. The joy of the Lord flows like a river. Even when I am confronted by many bills, the joy of the Lord makes me strong and hopeful that things are going to be alright.

I vividly remember that Dad had to wait for me to do certain things. One day, I got home from school, and I took Dad out to buy groceries at a nearby store. This was always difficult, as he was blind, and I was still a young boy.

And I thought to myself, "When would this suffering end?" My mother was a housewife. Other than her dedication to her farming labour, she had no other professional positions. With farming, she had to work hard to feed us, just as Dad had to wait for weeks to get his pension paid. Mum was busy growing groundnuts, cassava leaves and roots, bananas, yams, and maize. After accumulating many sacks of groundnuts, Mum could bring groundnuts home. We used groundnuts in two ways: for daily eating and for sale. Eating groundnuts was my favorite.

To this day, while overseas, I am nostalgic for the porridge "Mbouata" we used to make from cassava roots and eat it with either boiled or roasted peanuts. When peanuts were half-cooked, they looked crunchy, which was my favourite way of having peanuts with Mbouata. However, I do enjoy Australian food. I didn't know that God existed until the age of 10, when I realised that my parents had been attending the Salvation Army Church. Dad and Mum were dedicated to attending Sunday services. One day, dad had excruciating pain in his eyes, and a spiritual man was brought home to pray for him and apply some traditional medicine, such as herbs. After prayer from the visiting spiritual man, dad felt better. However, my father never recovered his health in the long run. Herbs had been used by my ancestors to heal certain sicknesses. But I couldn't remember if prayers and medicine (from plants or pharmacies) went together.

As a child, I knew nothing about prayer and thought that any person could have the power to heal the sick regardless of the person's belief, whether Christian, Hindu, Muslim, or even atheist. One thing I've noticed is that children tend to mimic their parents' actions and beliefs. And this can have a huge impact on the children's lives.

Proverbs 11:29

"He who directs his house badly exposes it to the wind."

The wind represents everything that happens to us or shakes us. Jesus Christ said that "our house must be built on the rock (Matthew 7:24)". Our house refers to our life too.

My parents were partly responsible for what was going on in our household, especially my constant mood swings. Although dad and mum were Christians, Bible study was not continuously conducted at home. There was no way that practical Christianity could have positively influenced my life. There was a spiritual vacuum that needed filling.

In that period, my two older sisters were already married. I think there was no ongoing spiritual oversight from the Salvation Army leadership, which was the local church in our hometown, Mossendjo. In this case, I see the role of the local church in overseeing or spiritually following up on the families in their community. Today, a common thing is that churches are filled with routine activities, ignoring some of the most critical pastoral duties, which include follow-ups. Some churches do follow up after each Sunday service, which is good for outreach. Churches must appoint pastoral teams to do the follow-up every week.

The prayer life was not practised with passion and faith in our home in Mossendjo. God said, "My house must be a house of prayer" (Matthew 21:13). Whoever is reading this, please make your house a prayer cell, and you will see what the Lord will do for you and your family. In my hometown, there was no Connect group on our street, so I couldn't even go to Bible studies.

I commenced primary education at the age of five in a public boys' school in Mossendjo. As the school fees were affordable, my parents could pay for the schoolbooks and tuition fees. During my elementary education, I had classes either in the morning or in the afternoon, depending on the weekly timetable. At the end of my morning classes, I used to go to the cassava and groundnut plantations, which were located about 2-3 kilometres from the city, to get my supplies because mum had to return home after 6 pm. That situation of going to the plantations with split timetables and any tardiness not being tolerated at my school made things a little bit tough.

When the Lord Jesus Christ was born, the Bible says he was not born into a wealthy family in Bethlehem. The Bible says, "Mary gave birth to a son, her firstborn. She wrapped him in swaddling clothes and laid him in a manger, because there was no room for them in the traveler's shelter (Luke 2:7).

The King of kings, the Lord of lords, was born in an environment that was not a cozy place, but which hid an immeasurable grandeur from the Savior of humanity. The manger was a place where food was placed to feed the cattle. It symbolised a low-class setting. It was the symbol of the humility of a king, our Lord Jesus Christ, who had been impoverished to enrich us. Bethlehem was not only the hometown of the Lord Jesus Christ but also the city where King David was anointed as King of Israel.

Chapter One: The Existence of God

For me, my childhood days were like gems. Gems are pebbles that have different colors, and they are found along riverbanks, beaches, and run-off channels. The abrasive power of running water exposes the internal colours of minerals in the rock pieces. So, gems shine because they have gone through a long process of erosion.

The gems are those lived experiences in my early years in primary and secondary school. For instance, one of my teachers punished me by requiring me to bring brooms for the daily cleaning of classrooms—a form of harsh discipline imposed on schoolboys. To make matters worse, I remember my late mother going out to cut some palm tree branches to make a broom for me because I was urged to bring a broom to school the following Monday.

In Africa, at least during our days, primary school teachers used to punish students severely to discipline them. So, students may be asked to write a statement like "I will never be late to school." Students were compelled to write such a statement 200 times on a piece of paper to earn a pardon from teachers. I cannot recall well what I did at school to deserve such a punishment as bringing a broom to school to sweep the floor of our classroom.

I accompanied mum to a river called "Makengue," where palm trees had grown up tall. She took a machete and cut some branches down. As I was looking on, her right arm got stuck between branches. Mum struggled bending the branches as she was less than 1.7 meters tall. As a child, I was helpless and continued to stare at her. At last, she grabbed a cluster of palm tree leaves. Unfortunately, mum got injured and her right hand started bleeding. She bandaged it with a piece of cloth and told me she had got the leaves, and we had to go home.

To me, that event was a gem in its own, as it reminds me of an unforgettable moment in my life. My mother was very supportive and caring. She took risks to make sure I got what I was looking for. By analogy, gems represent memorable times that left scars on us. I believe that the scars we get on our skin recall essential events or moments in a person's life. On my nose, there is a small scar that always reminds me of the chickenpox I had. Although we do remember the tough times in life, the Bible tells us not to dwell on our past (Isaiah 43:18).

Life has three phases: the past, the present, and the future. We cannot detach ourselves from these times as they shape our lives. The past marks our memory lanes that we reflect upon now and then. At times, we may not remember all the moments, but the mental scars cannot be undone at once.

Hebrews 12:2

"Let's keep our eyes focused on Jesus, who is the author and the finisher of our faith".

It is through the triumphal victory of Jesus at Calvary that our faith is born. I know that God has always provided the best outcome for me when I go through stuff. Things we go through may be good or bad, but they are meant for a purpose so that God's plan is revealed by shaping us through circumstances. I don't know what took place the day I was born, but I know I was cared for. We should have the attitude of knowing that we are wrapped up in God's arms. God protects us as a mother hen protects her chicks (Psalm 91:4).

On the day I was born, I guess I could hardly see light in the room where I was resting well-wrapped in a warm cotton

Chapter One: The Existence of God

blanket. My guess is that there were birds behind the house. I could feel the touch of the tender hands of my mother and the whisper of a song celebrating the birth of a long-awaited son. My mother had me ten years after giving birth to my older sister.

There was persistence and a never-give-up attitude. I believe that my late father would have walked into the maternity ward and taken a deep breath before touching and kissing me, the newborn. Mom's heart, I imagined, was beating with diastolic and systolic rhythms dictated by the baby's movements on her laps. Coming out of my mother's womb, my feet came out first and my head came out last.

Most children are born with their heads coming out first and their feet last. Mine was the opposite. My view is that I wanted my feet to touch the ground first. I was born to advance, not go backwards. Thank God! Even at my birth, God set me apart from other children. I am unique, and no one is like me on the entire planet Earth. I want to encourage you and tell you that you are incomparable, irreplaceable, indispensable, incredible, intelligent, and indomitable—there is no situation God cannot turn around.

In the seemingly quiet maternity room, the heavens were open for a child born into the Makoundi family. My destiny was already set and started to unfold right there. Although forces of all kinds were gravitating around the room, God's finger was pointing to the little child, which was me. The baby's first week on Earth was filled with laughter, and the frequency of it never ends. Whenever visitors started flocking into the maternity unit room, they saw that the child was different from other children born on the same day.

In the place where the child was born, there were three rivers that met: the river of gratitude, the river of fruitfulness, and the river of God's grace. The baby's life had always been full of colors, miracles, and untapped potentials available at God's discretion. The trajectory of the baby's life has been knitted, moving around hills and valleys that are constantly flattened by God's unlimited grace. Wherever we find ourselves, God's grace makes our climbing easier and effortless.

Psalm 146: 9

"The Lord watches over the refugees, he raises the widow and the orphan, but he defeats the plans of the wicked."

Before I take you into the next chapter, let me say that there is something called a worldview or culture that often impacts our upbringing. The point I am making here is that "do we always see the things God sees?" - The straight answer is no. Many times, when God points us towards victory related to His promises, we tend to contemplate defeat. When I was growing up, I practiced some forms of spirituality. For example, in my culture, we can stop the rain by simply putting a coin in a glass of water and then placing it on top of any hut's roof. The clouded sky would clear swiftly. I thought the forces of nature could be controlled by using cultural practices. But that is not what the Bible commands us to do.

Tools such as prayer, faith, and the declaration of God's promises are sufficient to control the forces of nature. In 1 Kings 17:1 and James 5:17, the Bible says Elijah was a human just like us; however, when he prayed earnestly that no rain would fall, none fell for three and a half years. When we pray, things can also happen. Let's keep prayer central in our lives. About worldview, Anderson and Goss (2009) stressed that we all have a worldview, which is the way we look at reality. We were taught that if you were born into a middle-class family with a cobbler father, you would end up doing the same job your father did. In some societies, the level of attainment of the parents limits that of their children. This cultural mindset is an antidote to faith in God.

Faith in God unleashes the power of God. Faith should transcend all cultural practices. In my humble opinion, it is our knowledge of God that should direct how we view the world or uphold some form of worldview that goes along with the Bible. Certain cultural practices hinder our walk with God. We should be careful what sort of cultural practices we embrace in life. I am not saying that all African cultural practices are bad; some are still relevant today and have immense moral values.

Golden points

- Look around you and see how God displays his existence.
- Caring mothers are heroes. They sacrifice for the benefit of their children. Here, I haven't forgotten the fathers. Fathers who are conscious of their children's wellbeing are heroes too.
- There is no one who is exactly like you. In you [the person], there is a "you" [the real you] that needs to open to God.

- Experiencing God on a personal level is the most precious thing in life.
- May the peace of God, which surpasses all understanding, be with you all. You are a seed that will grow and become a tree, on which birds will rest. You were created as a unique person, different from others.

CHAPTER TWO

CHALLENGES ARE PART OF EVERYDAY LIFE

Frequently, we think that storms are to be taken out of the equation of walking with God. In fact, we are all enrolled in the school of challenges if we live in this world. The truth is that no one is immune to challenges. Challenges come and go, and that is life.

Calming a storm

> *Mark 4: 35-41 (NIV)*
>
> [35] *That day when evening came, he (Jesus) said to his disciples, "Let us go over to the other side."* [36] *Leaving the crowd behind, they took him along, just as he was, in the boat. There were also other boats with him.* [37] *A furious squall came up, and the waves broke over the boat, so that it was nearly swamped.* [38] *Jesus was in the boat, sleeping on a*

> cushion. The disciples woke him and said to him, "Teacher, don't you care if we drown?"
>
> ³⁹ He got up, rebuked the wind, and said to the waves, "Quiet! Be still!" Then the wind died down and it was completely calm. ⁴⁰ He said to his disciples, "Why are you so afraid? Do you still have no faith?" ⁴¹ They were terrified and asked each other, "Who is this? Even the wind and the waves obey him!"

One of the things I have discovered in my journey with God is how badly we can be affected by the storms that keep hitting us as we fight the good fight of faith. Wherever you are on Earth, remember that there will be storms that will come your way from different directions and potentially make your life unstable. Some storms are caused by people who live in our immediate surroundings or are triggered by the way we live our lives. Some storms can come out of the blue.

For instance, some storms are generated within your own family. Family members can be agents of storms.

Let's look at Genesis 37: 12-17 from the Amplified Bible version.

> ¹² Now his brothers went to pasture their father's flock near Shechem. ¹³ Israel (Jacob) said to Joseph, "Are not your brothers pasturing [the flock] at Shechem? Come, and I will send you to them." And he said, "Here I am [ready to obey you]." ¹⁴ Then Jacob said to him, "Please go and see whether everything is all right with your brothers and all right with the flock; then bring word

> *[back] to me." So, he sent him from the Hebron Valley, and he went to Shechem.*
> *¹⁵ Now a certain man found Joseph and saw that he was wandering around and had lost his way in the field; so, the man asked him, "What are you looking for?" ¹⁶ He said, "I am looking for my brothers. Please tell me where they are pasturing our flocks." ¹⁷ Then the man said, "[They were here, but] they have moved on from this place. I heard them say, 'Let us go to Dothan.'" So, Joseph went after his brothers and found them at Dothan.*

Verse 12 starts with Joseph, who was living his normal life. It appears that Joseph was getting along well with his siblings. That is the reason why his father could send him to go meet with his brothers. Joseph found his brothers in Dothan.

The Plot against Joseph: how did it all happen?

The plot against Joseph was a massive storm in Joseph's life. The storm originated from the hatred his brothers had against him. He was hated for nothing. Joseph did nothing to deserve such treatment. I believe that was the work of the devil to just create a sense of hatred to intentionally dislike someone. One of the best weapons the devil is using is to divide family members by fuelling hatred in people's hearts. In fact, hatred is even more dangerous than anger. Anger can subside, but hatred is far more devastating to individuals. Hatred deeply affects our mental health (Chabra et al., 2014).

Siblings conspired to do evil

Genesis 37: 18-20

¹⁸ And when they saw him from a distance, even before he came close to them, they plotted to kill him. ¹⁹ They said to one another, "Look, here comes this dreamer. ²⁰ Now then, come and let us kill him and throw him into one of the pits (cisterns, underground water storage); then we will say [to our father], 'A wild animal killed and devoured him'; and we shall see what will become of his dreams!"

From verse 18 to verse 20, we see how Joseph's brothers had the thought to have him killed. Literally, Joseph's brothers were dream killers. They wanted to kill him for what he had. You can be victimised for your gifts, talents, and achievements.

Research showed that hatred works like poison (Brudholm and Lang, 2018). Hate is a mighty, strong, and negative feeling. It is a mental poison that can spoil your mind, soul, and spirit. When it becomes intense, it can take someone into a state of depression and even induce suicidal thoughts.

Hatred can end in ungodly actions

Genesis 37:21-24

²¹ Now Reuben [the eldest] heard this and rescued Joseph from their hands and said, "Let us not take his life." ²² Reuben said to them, "Do not shed his

> blood, but [instead] throw him [alive] into the pit that is here in the wilderness, and do not lay a hand on him [to kill him]"—[he said this so] that he could rescue him from them and return him [safely] to his father. ²³ Now when Joseph reached his brothers, they stripped him of his tunic, the [distinctive] multi-coloured tunic which he was wearing; ²⁴ then they took him and threw him into the pit. Now the pit was empty; there was no water in it.

Hatred is dangerous and can lead to irreparable consequences. During the plot against Joseph, Reuben had a different thought than his brothers, which resulted in an ungodly act. What I can say here is that no matter what you will go through or have gone through, God can graciously position you like Reuben. All your enemies' vices against you will be aborted or thwarted by God. God watches over our lives even in death-and-life situations. Can we all say Amen?

The consummation of hate-motivated action

Genesis 37: 25-26

> ²⁵ Then they sat down to eat their meal. When they looked up, they saw a caravan of Ishmaelites coming from Gilead [east of the Jordan], with their camels bearing ladanum resin [for perfume] and balm and myrrh, going on their way to carry the cargo down to Egypt. ²⁶ Judah said to his brothers,

> *"What do we gain if we kill our brother and cover up his blood (murder)?*

This passage demonstrates how Judah pondered what his brothers were planning. We must constantly reflect on our intentions to see if they are pleasing to God. The Bible says this in Philippians 4:8. Finally, brothers and sisters, whatever is true, whatever is noble, whatever is right, whatever is pure, whatever is lovely, whatever is admirable—if anything is excellent or praiseworthy—think about such things.

In our lives, we should ask God to help us have thoughts that are pure. The word "pure" can mean uncontaminated. A child of God needs to give more space to the Holy Spirit to do the work of filtering our thoughts to release only those that are honorable. I had been in situations where my thoughts were contaminated. And I prayed to God to help me fight them—not by my own strength but with the aid of the Holy Ghost.

I clearly remember having encountered two women: one in a taxicab and another at a government office in Malaysia. Cab drivers used to pick up people on the streets and drop them off at their respective stops based on how much each customer paid for a trip.

The woman I met in a cab gave a thought-provoking statement. She stated that no man in this world is faithful (meaning he does not cheat on his wife). She said men cannot live without having another concubine, excluding their wives. She added that men have been made just like that. While the cab was still moving and I was sitting on her right side, I felt a bombshell of itchy words penetrating my ears. I could not hold myself and reacted quickly before my stop. I told her that what you just said does not apply to every man because I am not the sort of unfaithful husband you may think I am. I was in my third year of marriage to my wife, who is still living with me to this day. The lady then looked straight at me and said you must be telling a lie.

You look handsome and cannot live with one woman; only she reacted. When I reached my stop, I asked the cab driver to drop me. I got out of the cab and began to ponder. I found it baseless, childish, and immature. I knew that in this world, people don't know that marriage is sacred. It all comes down to having the fear of God. The fear of God is the beginning of wisdom. When we fear God, there are things we are not permitted to do or even assist others to do.

The second woman I met in Malaysia knew me as one of the members of the African community. She must have known my wife. She came over to where I was standing and asked me with a gentle voice, "Charles, are you faithful to your wife?" That was something I never thought she would ask me. I lifted my eyes, and with no hesitation, I said, "Why do you ask me such a question?" She smiled and snapped back by saying, "Charles, why can't you answer my question?" I said to her, "I am faithful to my wife." I turned down her advances and walked away.

Genesis 37: 27-36

> [27] *Come, let us [instead] sell him to these Ishmaelites [and Midianites] and not lay our hands on him, because he is our brother and our flesh." So, his brothers listened to him and agreed.* [28] *Then as the Midianite [and Ishmaelite] traders were passing by, the brothers pulled Joseph up and lifted him*

out of the pit, and they sold him to the Ishmaelites for twenty shekels of silver. And so, they took Joseph [as a captive] into Egypt.

²⁹ Now Reuben [unaware of what had happened] returned to the pit, and [to his great alarm found that] Joseph was not in the pit; so, he tore his clothes [in deep sorrow]. ³⁰ He rejoined his brothers and said, "The boy is not there; as for me, where shall I go [to hide from my father]?" ³¹ Then they took Joseph's tunic, slaughtered a male goat and dipped the tunic in the blood; ³² and they brought the multi-coloured tunic, to their father, saying, "We have found this; please examine it and decide whether or not it is your son's tunic." ³³ He recognized it and said, "It is my son's tunic. A wild animal has devoured him; Joseph is without doubt torn in pieces!" ³⁴ So Jacob tore his clothes [in grief], put on sackcloth and mourned many days for his son. ³⁵ Then all his sons and daughters attempted to console him, but he refused to be comforted and said, "I will go down to Sheol (the place of the dead) in mourning for my son." And his father wept for him. ³⁶ Meanwhile, in Egypt the Midianites sold Joseph [as a slave] to Potiphar, an officer of Pharaoh and the captain of the [royal] guard.

Drawing some parallels to the way Jacob felt and how Joseph acted, it turns out that the heart of Jacob is comparable to the heart of our Heavenly Father. He grieved after knowing that his son may have died. God turned what was meant for evil into good in Joseph's life.

Never turn your anger into an act of violence

Once upon a time, I faced a storm when one of my cousins began to quarrel with me in front of my late mother. He threatened to turn his back on me for a problem that had no connection to me. He wanted to hide his wrongdoings by exposing me as the scapegoat. Suddenly, anger flared up in my heart, and I went into my bedroom to cry and perhaps control myself. My mother noticed that I had lost control and wanted to get even and fight with my cousin. She called me privately and asked me to cool down. I thank God that I came to my senses and slept well that night. Every day, when you wake up, stand on the promises of God, and despite the power of the wind, you can hold onto Jesus, and he will always provide a way out when facing a disaster of any kind.

Always starts your day with God

One evening, Jesus spoke with his disciples (Mark 4:35). In this verse, the disciples did not know that they would face a strong storm later. The only thing they knew was that God had set them on a journey with Him. I have discovered in life that as I walk with God, that voyage is not "challenge-free." There will always be trials and tests as we walk with God. In fact, God is all-knowing, and Jesus, our Lord, foresees what lies ahead of us. However, going through unchartered territories is likely to happen. Sometimes, we want God to lead us in a way that meets our expectations. When I started my Christian journey, I had these fancy thoughts that God's blessings were tied to my thoughts all the time. But it is God's thoughts towards us that prevail. We even argue with God so that the journey he has planned for us can be mutually agreed upon.

Jesus did not ask the disciples their opinion about going to the other side of the lake with the expectation of encountering a storm. Jesus said authoritatively, "Let's go to the other side." Jesus knew they would hit a storm, but they went anyway! You may be in a difficult situation; you look very reluctant about whether to act or not. In a similar vein, should I obey God or listen to the voice of my flesh? God is the captain of our boat. Therefore, we just need to obey him and go wherever he leads us.

Leaving the crowd behind - Mark 4: 36

Our salvation is personal. Learning to know God personally is our responsibility and a choice. The disciples left the crowd behind and stayed with Jesus. We genuinely grow in God when we make Him our friend. Although churches have Bible teaching series to help Christians know God more deeply, this practice does not complete the divine modeling, or the shape He (God) intends for us. God does the shaping. As it says, God is the potter, and we are the clay (Isaiah 64:8).

We must have quality time with God. An example of time spent with God could be the worship service one morning at your church or during Bible study; however, quality time is the amount of time invested in every conversation with God. This conversation is a two-way road.

Ten years of church attendance does not make someone a disciple of Jesus Christ. You become one when you begin to put into practice His teachings (John 8:31–32). We must surrender all and make room for God to lead us. It is your revelation of God that will see you through difficult times. Peter got it right, when asked who Jesus was. And Peter answered, "You are the Christ, the son of the living God" (Matthew 16:13–20). Nevertheless, Apostle Peter struggled to know the ways of God (Matthew 26:31–35).

Moses also found that leading the people of God out of Egypt was a "hard act to follow." He went from excuse to excuse just to avoid the God-given assignment. Moses spent 40 days on Mount Sinai to receive the Ten Commandments. God didn't shorten his stay on the mountain. There is a price to pay if we want to grow in our knowledge of God. Elijah when threatened by Jezebel told God he wanted to take his own life (1 Kings 19: 1-4). Naaman was asked to dip into the "dirty" Jordan River seven times to get rid of his leprosy (2 Kings 5: 9-15). Never question God; he has better plans for you (Jeremiah 29: 11).

Mystery of divine care is beyond human intelligence - Mark 4: 37

We can hardly comprehend the mystery of God's care in our lives. Have you ever asked why God allowed certain things to happen in your life? Once upon a time, I travelled to do fieldwork with one of my university professors, who happened to be a Christian. This man loved God. Every day, I saw him reading the Bible and praying to God. One day, he got the bad news that his wife had been seriously injured in a car crash when she was heading to the airport to travel overseas. He took a break and went back to his hometown to visit his family and check on the situation on the ground. I asked a straightforward question, "Why did God allow that to happen to him?" "Why do some good people suffer a lot?"

You are probably facing a difficult time as you read this book. I want to assure you that God is in control. In Mark 4:37, a storm severely battered the boat in which Jesus and the disciples were traveling. When hit by a storm, we often think that God has abandoned us. We have the impression of trying to find answers on our own without God's backing. Furthermore, the fact that God is not physically present makes us feel vulnerable, as if Heaven is tightly shut. In the book of Genesis, the Bible says that the Israelites were forced to labour for the Egyptians for nearly 430 years. Exodus 2:25 tells us, "So God looked on the Israelites and was concerned about them."

And Pharaoh, the king of Egypt at the time, feared the Israelites' growing presence. The Israelites were in limbo and could not find a way out of their terrible enslavement. God waited for His own timing to mightily deliver the Israelites out of slavery.

The psalmist said that God is a refuge for the oppressed, a refuge in times of trouble (Psalm 9:9). It means that despite the nature of your problems, God is still present right where you are.

Chapter Two: Challenges are Part of Everyday Life

Financial difficulties

The story of the paralyzed man at the gate called Beautiful.

Acts 3: 1-8

> *¹one-day Peter and John were going up to the temple at the time of prayer-at three in the afternoon. ² Now a man who was lame from birth was being carried to the temple gate called Beautiful, where he was put every day to beg from those going into the temple courts. ³ When he saw Peter and John about to enter, he asked them for money. ⁴ Peter looked straight at him, as did John. Then Peter said, "Look at us!" ⁵ So the man gave them his attention, expecting to get something from them (Acts 3: 1-5). ⁶Then Peter said "silver or gold I do not have, but what I have I give you. In the name of Jesus Christ of Nazareth, walk". ⁷Taking him by the right hand, he helped him up, and instantly the man's feet and ankles became strong. ⁸He jumped to his feet and began to walk.*

From this story, the paralyzed man asked for money which he did not get. But God did a miracle which I believe is far more significant than what the man was looking for. His physical condition changed on the spot, and he began to walk which he was unable to do since his birth.

The experience of Hannah

There was a certain man from Ramathaim, a Zuphite from the hill country of Ephraim, whose name was Elkanah son of Jeroham, the son of Elihu, the son of Tohu, the son of Zuph, an Ephraimite. [2] He had two wives; one was called Hannah and the other Peninnah. Peninnah had children, but Hannah had none (1 Samuel 1: 1-2). This situation made Hannah look inferior in front of Peninnah, but God blessed Hannah with a God-fearing son, Samuel.

We should not look down on others because each one of us has a unique identity. Every person is born with an intrinsic value that makes each human different from every other human. The person you neglect today might help you out tomorrow.

We are social and relational beings

In the Bible, Moses was a leader like Joshua, but he was the one that God used to lead people through the Red Sea. Joshua was a totally different person; he had the ability to not only take the baton from Moses but also lead across the Jordan River. For example, in a relay race, people team up for a single purpose. When athletes are on the same team, they cooperate. For example, the first runner holds the baton in their right hand; the second runner holds the baton in their left hand; the third runner takes and holds the baton in their right hand; and the fourth runner takes and holds the baton in their left hand. They all try to win a prize.

What I know is that to win a relay race, athletes pass the baton to teammates by not using the same hand position. God told me here that even in accomplishing his purpose on Earth, we should not live in isolation—no one is an island! What I have to say here is that to win, every team member needs to cooperate and think of the other team member.

Priesthood duties

Joshua had the ability to positively influence the priests on how to carry the Ark of the Covenant, which represented the presence of God. The word Ark comes from the Latin word "arca," which means big box. The box contained sacred things precious to God, symbolising the presence of God as the Israelites wandered in the desert after their deliverance from slavery in Egypt. No one could look at or even touch the Ark when it was uncovered. In the Ark were the Ten Commandments, a pot full of manna (food God provided to the Israelites in the desert), and the stuff belonging to Moses' brother Aaron. The Ark guided the people of God on their way to the Promised Land.

Joshua listened to the voice of God. He knew when God was speaking. He told the Israelites what God told him. Even the way we carry out our spiritual tasks can be challenging.

Discouragement

Sometimes, we may be affected by discouragement that could damage our reputation or self-esteem. The story in Genesis

29:25 tells us that Jacob was deceived by his father-in law. At some point, Jacob decided to get married. Jacob left Haran and travelled to Paddan Aram to find a wife. Over there, he met with Laban, who was his relative. Prior to meeting Rachel, who was a shepherdess working for her father Laban, Jacob felt the need to look for his relatives.

The way the events unfolded was amazing. Jacob arrived in the eastern region of Paddan Aram and met with its inhabitants. Jacob had an opportunity that opened a door for him. The circumstances of getting a wife were not pleasing, and Jacob was deceived by his potential father-in law. Jacob and Laban had a deal. Jacob agreed to work for seven years before taking Rachel as his wife.

After those years, Jacob was presented with Leah, Rachel's older sister, as a wife. There was deep dissatisfaction from Jacob, and he was forced to serve another seven years to finally secure Rachel as his wife. Every time I read this story of Jacob; it moves my heart. Jacob never had the intention of taking both daughters from Laban. He ended up having seven children with Leah and two with Rachel. Among the children of Rachel was Joseph, the firstborn from Rachel's womb. After escaping the tragic event of nearly being killed by his own brothers, Joseph was born as a star and went on to become Egypt's second-in-command.

Jacob was forced to work for another 7 years to obtain Rachel. The story went on to say that after a long period of barrenness, Rachel became pregnant and bore a child called Joseph. In life, stick to what you believe is reasonable to pursue. We can see that Joseph was not an ordinary child who came after a long struggle. I have found out that in life, great things happen when we have gone through some turbulence.

Chapter Two: Challenges are Part of Everyday Life

Struggles are like pipelines in which we are refined and come out of them pure like gold. Struggles augment our values in this world. Most biblical figures who went through many struggles impacted their generations. A part of Daniel's life speaks volume in the way we should trust God in the midst of adversity.

Daniel 6: 16-23

16. So the king gave the order, and they brought Daniel and threw him into the lions' den. The king said to Daniel, "May your God, whom you serve continually, rescue you!"
17. A stone was brought and placed over the mouth of the den, and the king sealed it with his own signet ring and with the rings of his nobles, so that Daniel's situation might not be changed. 18 Then the king returned to his palace and spent the night without eating and without any entertainment being brought to him. And he could not sleep.
19. At the first light of dawn, the king got up and hurried to the lions' den. 20. When he came near the den, he called to Daniel in an anguished voice, "Daniel, servant of the living God, has your God, whom you serve continually, been able to rescue you from the lions?"
21. Daniel answered, "May the king live forever! 22. My God sent his angel, and he shut the mouths of the lions. They have not hurt me, because

> *I was found innocent in his sight. Nor have I ever done any wrong before you, Your Majesty."*
>
> *23. The king was overjoyed and gave orders to lift Daniel out of the den. And when Daniel was lifted from the den, no wound was found on him, because he had trusted in his God.*

Daniel didn't make any concessions to the King's requests while he was in Babylon. Daniel would rather submit to God than a monarch on earth. All of this was taking place in the backdrop of Daniel refusing to pray to or worship the King of Babylon. He continued to pray three times each day as he had in the past. The fact that Daniel disobeyed the King made him feel ashamed. Daniel was to be thrown into the lions' den, per the King's command. Throwing someone into lions' dens was cruel and inhumane. Daniel went through excruciating hardships from which only God could deliver him. Because Daniel believed God, God did it.

First instincts matter in life

Let me explain how I met my wife. One afternoon in my home country, I was going for a walk in the Moungali suburb of Brazzaville. It happened in 1989, when I saw a young woman, beautifully dressed, who was walking on the right side of the road. She looked thoughtful and indifferent to the onlookers. I gazed at her and was prompted to stop her. That was a thunderbolt!

I asked her if she could take a few minutes for a quick chat with me. She responded calmly that she was in a hurry and wanted to go home to rest after a long, busy day at university. She needed to get home as she was returning from a university lecture. However, she noted my home address on a piece of paper so that she might pay me a visit at her own convenience.

It took a long time—at least five months since I met her. I was renting a small apartment to be close to my university's campus. She came to see me unexpectedly, and luckily or fortuitously I was home at that time. Lucky boy! She entered my apartment and did not even sit down. She said she was running late and that she was satisfied to know where I lived. She disappeared for at least four months and came to visit me in another place.

Everything started from that day, and she went on to be my life companion until this day. Today, I cannot regret having this beautiful being as my wife, friend, and spiritual partner.

Proverbs 18:22

"He who finds a wife finds a good thing."

I believe I was guided by God to land this wonderful lady, who is my wife, to do life together. Finding a soul mate is very important in life. What I want to say is that my wife accepted me just as I was in those days. It will take more than ten books to write about how I felt when I first met my wife.

Close to giving up

Mark 4: 37

A furious squall came up, and the waves broke over the boat, so that it was nearly swamped.

When the water began to rise and flood the boat, Jesus was in it. This is what happens in our lives when we think that we are losing all hope. At times, we have tried it all, but nothing has worked. This is also a time when we nearly "give up." The disciples thought they were going to drown. Let's pause here: God is ever-present through hard times. He is never out of touch. Many of us probably want to give up due to a lack of understanding of things occurring around us. Job had a weird lived experience when he lost most of his possessions, and his children (Job 1:1-22).

Job did not understand why he suffered so much. There will be a lot of testing in life. Our trust in God will rise to a higher degree when we pass some tests of faith.

What God does is always beyond our comprehension. We cannot know why God allows each incident or storm to come into our lives, nor do we know the benefits of going through trials. Testing is often painful; however, the outcome is great. Job never gave up, and God blessed him with a double portion of what he lost. Our road with God is not always a "tarred road."

Our journey with God comprises different phases, and only God knows the ups and downs. Sometimes, the road may be sandy, muddy, swampy, mountainous, frosty, thorny, and pebbly. God used the Red Sea to communicate with his children. He made Joseph pass through Potiphar's house and get tempted by his wife. Although he committed no crime, Joseph was put in jail. He ended up being the prime minister of Egypt. The Bible tells us God makes all things work together for our good (Romans 8:28). And he does.

Jesus never promised that whatever path we take would be devoid of challenges. If such a teaching exists, it is purely utopian. God does promise triumph through adversity.

God does not panic when we do

Mark 4: 36-41

> [36] *Leaving the crowd behind, they took him along, just as he was, in the boat. There were also other boats with him.* [37] *A furious squall came up, and the waves broke over the boat, so that it was nearly swamped.* [38] *Jesus was in the stern, sleeping on a cushion. The disciples woke him and said to him, "Teacher, don't you care if we drown?"*
>
> [39] *He got up, rebuked the wind, and said to the waves, "Quiet! Be still!" Then the wind died down and it was completely calm.*
>
> [40] *He said to his disciples, "Why are you so afraid? Do you still have no faith?"*
>
> [41] *They were terrified and asked each other, "Who is this? Even the wind and the waves obey him!"*

There are two categories of people from a spiritual perspective. Those who have faith in God and those who do not have faith in God—with this, there is no middle ground. Oftentimes, when our faith is shaken by problems, we tend to lose all hope. When our faith is tested, God is not shaken. As God sits on His throne, He looks down from Heaven and places us in less disastrous circumstances, so that when we emerge from the storm, we can finally say that it was God's action.

As Jesus was asleep the disciples woke him up and said don't you care Lord if we drown? God's attitude was different from that of his disciples. During a storm, the Lord Jesus was asleep. When our world is shaken, just lay down your head on Jesus. He is our place of peace, joy, protection, and provision.

Nothing is constant

I have been living in Australia for over 13 years. The ever-changing nature of the weather has always been the thing that has struck me the most since I arrived. There are four seasons in a year, making me believe that nothing is constant. In Tasmania, four seasons can occur in a day, which is even more surprising to me. I've learned to bring my sweater with me wherever I go. Acclimatizing in Tasmania took me a while.

It is much the same if someone lives in an area where there are two seasons in a year, the warm and cold seasons, much like the weather in my home country. So, things keep changing, and we try to get used to the dynamics of life. There is a reflection I came up with, which is the relationship between perception of day-to-day life and adaptability: "Adaptability = reality x perception." Every single day we live is a reality of things that we go through, some of which are likeable, and others are not. Regardless of the case, we often face reality every single day. What shapes us is our adaptability as to how we perceive or deal with our daily struggles. In other words, the way things are amplified by circumstantial realities directly influences our level of adaptability or resilience in life.

Things you cannot control

Life is full of surprises, and you cannot control what might happen next. You only need to commit every step you take to God and leave the future entirely in God's caring hands. What I have been through has caused me to even question God about the significance of life. The constant answer I got from God was that "life is found in Him." Without God, there is no life. God has the power to take away the breath of life or to bring any dead thing back to life.

The Bible says that it has been appointed for man to live once, then comes death. People are doomed to die once and then face judgement (Hebrews 9:27). I am not afraid of death because I know I will be welcomed by my Father in Heaven when my journey on Earth comes to an end. I have experienced some tough times, and I learned a lot from them. In 2010, I was in Malaysia. A couple of months before coming to Australia, I received the bad news that my mother had died. It was early in the morning, and I was on my way to work. To control myself, I did not inform the driver of the ordeal until we reached our destination. I took one day off to be alone and try to digest the pain I was bearing. I was far from my home country, and I was unable to arrange things to make it to the

Congo for mum's burial. I came to learn that the passing of a loved one can be a painful experience, but that's life. In such circumstances, we should find comfort in God, who is there for us twenty-four hours a day, seven days a week.

One thing is that any negative event in our lives has an unfathomable side effect. That side is a mystery that only God knows. No matter the level of the anointing, we cannot take the place of the Holy Spirit. We are guided by the Holy Spirit in whatever we do.

> *Isaiah 11:1-3 refers to Jesus Christ, our Lord. This passage reads in verse 2, "The Spirit of the Lord shall rest upon Him (Jesus), the Spirit of wisdom and understanding, the Spirit of counsel and might, the Spirit of knowledge and of the fear of the Lord.*

When we are baptised by the Holy Spirit, wisdom, understanding, counsel, might, knowledge, and the fear of God are given to us.

In the book of Joshua, when Moses died, God told Joshua to lead his people. God told Joshua to "be strong and very courageous" to lead the Israelites up to the Promised Land. Please note that Joshua's leadership was marked by the fall of Jericho's wall, whereas Moses' leadership was characterised by the parting of the Red Sea. Moses and Joshua were two different leaders, with two distinct assignments, and in two different environmental conditions. Joshua was anointed in the same way that Moses was to carry out the divine duties entrusted to him.

I also did not have the opportunity to attend dad's funeral. It took some time for Jesus to heal me of all my internal wounds. And now I am totally healed. In our relationships with people, you cannot control what others are going to say to you, but you can control what you are going to say to them or the way you respond to certain situations. It is not about how much has been said about you; it is more about how you respond to certain situations. The way we react to a situation determines the outcome of what we are going to get out of it.

The story of Abel and Cain

Genesis 4: 1-7.

> *¹Adam made love to his wife Eve, and she became pregnant and gave birth to Cain. She said, "With the help of the Lord, I have brought forth a man." ² Later she gave birth to his brother Abel. Now Abel kept flocks, and Cain worked the soil. ³ In the course of time Cain brought some of the fruits of the soil as an offering to the Lord. ⁴ Abel brought fat portions from some of the firstborn of his flock. The Lord looked with favor on Abel and his offering, ⁵ but on Cain and his offering he did not look with favor. So, Cain was very angry, and his face was downcast.⁶Then the LORD said to Cain, "Why are you angry? Why is your face downcast? ⁷If you do what is right, will you not be accepted? But if you do not do what is right, sin is crouching*

> *at your door; it desires to have you, but you must rule over it."*

God was impressed by Abel's gift, and he did not look at Cain's gift with a good impression. What we can learn from this story is that God's heart is moved when our offering is made with good intentions. Whatever the reason, anything we do in the Kingdom of God must be done without a string attached to it. It appears that the content of Cain's heart was not right at the time of giving.

We should not be envious of those who perform feats or are on top of the world in life. Envy is neither an attribute of the gift of God nor is it an element of the fruit of the Holy Spirit. Let's remind ourselves to always do good. When we do things the right way, God will always be pleased by our actions. In the same way, the quality of services we render is determined by the state of our hearts.

The motivations that drive our work will determine our success. God sees how and why we invest time in His work, and He will grant us success in all our endeavors. The point is that diligence in the things of God pays off.

Genesis 4: 8-10

> *[8] Now Cain said to his brother Abel, "Let's go out to the field." While they were in the field, Cain attacked his brother Abel and killed him.*
>
> *[9] Then the* LORD *said to Cain, "Where is your brother Abel?"*
>
> *"I don't know," he replied. "Am I my brother's keeper?"*

Chapter Two: Challenges are Part of Everyday Life

> *¹⁰And He said, "What have you done? The voice of your brother's blood cries out to me from the ground".*

The blood of a deceased person can speak. When we take an ungodly step to kill someone or have him or her killed, we are deceiving ourselves, and God will always be the defender of an innocent person. Never ever kill a human being. No one has the right to take another person's life. Harming someone to satisfy our ego is not the solution to our frustration. It simply demonstrates how vulnerable we are and how dangerous we have become in society.

Golden points

- Never allow ill thoughts to turn into hateful behavior.
- Never let the sun go down on your anger.
- Being happy is a choice.
- Always leave in God's hands that of which we have no understanding.

Chapter Three

God Still Does Miracles

God has not changed. The God who saved the Israelites from slavery in Egypt thousands of years ago is still the same as I write today. The way the Israelites crossed the Red Sea, leaving Egypt and thus ending decades of slavery, was phenomenal. This biblical passage shows how the Israelites were daydreaming about their freedom from harsh labour in Egypt.

Exodus 14:1–7

1) Now the Lord spoke to Moses, saying, 2) "tell the sons of Israel to turn back and camp in front of Pi-hahiroth, between Migdol and the sea. You shall camp in front of Baal-zephon, opposite it, by the sea. 3) For Pharaoh will say of the Israelites, "They are wandering aimlessly in the land; the wilderness has shut them in." 4) I will harden (make stubborn, defiant) Pharaoh's heart, so l will pursue them; and I will be glorified and honored through Pharaoh and all his army, and the Egyptians shall know [without any doubt] and acknowledge that I am the Lord." And they did so.

5) When the king of Egypt was told that the people had fled, Pharaoh and his servants had a change of heart toward the people, and they said, "What is this that we have done? We have let Israel go from serving us!" 6) So Pharaoh harnessed horses to his war-chariots [for battle] and took his army with him; 7) and he took six hundred chosen war-chariots, and all the other war-chariots of Egypt with fighting charioteers over all of them.

From verse 1 to 4, we see that God never shares his glory with anyone. As the Israelites were wandering in the desert, God swiftly acted in a chaotic situation to prove that He is Almighty and that all the forces of nature obey Him. In our daily struggles, God will never let us down when we call on Him. Call on Jesus when you are desperate, and He will surely rescue you and intervene in your case. If Pharaoh was wise enough, he would have let the Israelites go.

Wisdom is a good thing because it helps us recognize our spiritual and social boundaries in any sphere of life. Fighting or causing havoc in the life of a people or someone who is backed by God is like walking through a mine field. It is going to blast at any time, and the troublemaker could be the only victim.

We also see an analogy in the Bible when Saul failed to recognize that he was not fit to offer sacrifices and that it was the duty of Prophet Samuel. In 1 Samuel 13: 8-13 "Samuel had told Saul, "Go down ahead of me to Gilgal. I will surely come down to you to sacrifice burnt offerings and fellowship offerings, but you must wait seven days until I come to you and tell you what you are to do." But Saul, worried that his whole army would leave him, offered the sacrifices himself, just before Samuel arrived. That was a serious mistake and a lack of wisdom. When we are unable to recognize that we are not within our rights and power to do certain things, but we choose to do them anyway clearly points to a deficit of wisdom.

Exodus 14:8-9

> *8) The Lord hardened the heart of Pharaoh, king of Egypt, and he pursued the Israelites, as they were leaving confidently and defiantly. 9) The Egyptians chased them with all the horses and war-chariots of Pharaoh, his horsemen, and his army, and they overtook them as they camped by the sea, beside Pi-hahiroth, in front of Ball-zephon.*

Pharaoh was a title of the kings of ancient Egypt. Those kings were both heads of states and religious leaders as they served as intermediaries between their gods and the Egyptian people. Pharaoh's understanding of who God was at that time was rather darkened by his religion. So, pharaoh was spiritually short-sighted, and he acted foolishly. The bottom line is religion blinds us but relationship with God enlightens us.

Fear that cripples our mind

Exodus 14:10-12

__10__) As Pharaoh approached, the Israelites looked up and saw the Egyptians marching after them, and they were very frightened; so, the Israelites cried out to the Lord. __11__) Then they said to Moses, "Is it because there are no graves in Egypt that you have taken us away to die in the wilderness? What is this that you have done to us by bringing us out of Egypt? __12__) Did we not say to you in Egypt, 'Leave us alone; let us serve the Egyptians?' For it would have been better for us to serve the Egyptians [as slaves] than to die in the wilderness."

As humans, we often cry out to soothe our melancholy. This is normal but it becomes abnormal when we do not get over it. This is the reason why Jesus Christ said to the disciples when the boat was sinking due to a severe storm "you of little faith" (Matthew 8:26).

We often make the mistake of keeping the status quo (i.e. the current situation) when God has decided differently. I had the fear of damaging my social profile if I had to follow Jesus Christ. For instance, I was like a celebrity among my peers when I was between 10 and 16 years old. I was a fan of world-class reggae musicians such as Peter Tosh, U-Roy, Lucky Dube, Bob Marley, and many more. I also had my own fans who applauded me every time I had to dance and perform tricks to feed my ego. One of my magical tricks was to bend my body and get the back of my head to touch the ground while dancing. People used to give me a big clap. I had to go around shopping malls to look for new releases of reggae hits. I didn't have the love for Christian music or Gospel songs.

One day, God visited me. I heard a voice say to me "Charles you have to destroy all your reggae CD's, DVDs, and cassette tapes and throw them in a bin". Without hesitation, I threw them all in a bin. To walk with God, we must get rid of some stuff. I learnt that the measure of transformation in our life is proportional to the level of obedience to God.

The miracle of a divided sea

Exodus 14: 13-14

> **13)** Then Moses said to the people, "Do not be afraid! Take your stand [be firm and confident and undismayed] and see the salvation of the Lord which He will accomplish for you today; for those Egyptians whom you have seen today, you will never see again. **14)** The Lord will fight for you while you [only need to] keep silent and remain calm."

In our life, the Red Sea can be any insurmountable situation. I want to ensure the readers here that God can break your Red Sea apart. Crying may not change things – but it relieves us from pain.

Chapter Three: God Still Does Miracles

Exodus 14: 15-16

15) The Lord said to Moses, "Why do you cry to me? Tell the sons of Israel to move forward [toward the sea].

16) As for you, lift your staff and stretch out your hand over the Sea and divide it, so that the sons of Israel may go through the middle of the Sea on dry land.

Here the word staff can also mean skills you may have and a certain ability that makes you unique. So, a staff can be a talent or something you do passionately, and effortlessly. It flows naturally. If you have noticed such a thing, then you have gotten a staff. There are things we do and have not been taught at schools. If you are in that space then please use it, as it is undoubtedly a gift from God.

Exodus 14: 17-20

17) As for me, hear this: I will harden the hearts of the Egyptians, and they will go in [the sea] after them; and I will be glorified and honored through Pharaoh and all his army, and his war-chariots and his horsemen. 18) And the Egyptians shall know [without any doubt] and acknowledge that I am the Lord, when I am glorified and honored through Pharaoh, through his war-chariots and his charioteers."

19) The angel of God, who had been going in front of the camp of Israel, and all the war

> *chariots were behind them. The pillar of the cloud moved from in front and stood behind them. 20) So, it came between the camp of Egypt and the camp of Israel. It was a cloud along with darkness [even by day to the Egyptians], but it gave light by night [to the Israelites]; so, one [army] did not come near the other all night.*

Some children of God rely on their riches, academic achievements, or businesses thinking - these things make them secure in a broader sense of the word. But it is not true. Anything can happen and take a bizarre turn in life.

Most Biblical Heroes were men of courage

Exodus 14: 21-25

> *21) Then Moses stretched out his hand over the sea; and the Lord swept the sea back by a strong east wind all that night and turned the seabed into dry land, and the waters were divided. 22) The Israelites went into the middle of the sea on dry land, and the waters formed a wall to them on their right hand and on their left.*
>
> *23) Then the Egyptians pursued them into the middle of the sea, even all Pharaoh's horses, his war-chariots, and his charioteers. 24) So, it happened at the early morning watch [before dawn], that the Lord looked down on the army of the Egyptians through the pillar of fire and cloud and*

put them in a state of confusion. 25) He made their chariot wheels hard to turn, and the chariots difficult to drive; so, the Egyptians said, "Let us flee from Israel, for the Lord is fighting for them against the Egyptians."

From verse 23 to 25, I note that the Egyptians were adamant and continued to plan evil against the children of God.

Follow exactly what God says to you

Exodus 14: 26-30

26) Then the Lord said to Moses, "Stretch out your hand over the sea so that the waters may come back over the Egyptians, on their war-chariots and their charioteers." 27) So Moses stretched out his hand over the sea, and the sea returned to its normal flow at sunrise; and the Egyptians retreated right into it [being met by the returning water]; so the Lord overthrew the Egyptians, and tossed them into the midst of the sea. 28) The waters returned and covered the chariots and the charioteers, and all the army of Pharaoh that had gone into the sea after them; not even one of them survived. 29) But the Israelites walked on dry land in the middle of the sea, and the waters formed a wall to them on their right hand and on their left. 30) The Lord saved Israel that day from the hand of the

> *Egyptians and Israel saw the Egyptians [lying] dead on the seashore.*

Sometimes, deliverance comes after a long struggle

Miracles are physical manifestations or events that defy the law of nature or are beyond explanation of known human knowledge or powers. The crossing of the Red Sea on dry ground was one of them. Miracles cannot be explained naturally. These are supernatural things that cannot be explained through logic or human reasoning.

Romans 8: 28-30

> *[28] And we know that in all things God works for the good of those who love him, who have been called according to his purpose. [29] For those God foreknew he also predestined to be conformed to the image of his Son, that he might be the firstborn among many brothers and sisters. [30] And those he predestined, he also called; those he called, he also justified; those he justified, he also glorified.*

Life is like a trajectory that has flat and bumpy sections. We do not know what is going to happen to us until an event prompts. But we certainly know that God goes ahead of us as leader and stays behind us as protector because God is omnipresent. Now when something bad happens to us we often have the impression that God is far away whereas He is not.

Chapter Three: God Still Does Miracles

God is our all-time helper in moments of troubles (Psalm 46:1). You are known to God before your birth. He formed you in your mother's womb and he knows your whereabouts day and night. As a child of God, you are predestined to walk just like Jesus Christ walked on this Earth. The walk of a child of God is not devoid of some challenges and we should be prepared for them as they come our way. The end of every trial connects us to God's unlimited glory. Many miracles occurred in my life and ministry. Below are just a few of them that I can remember.

Delivered from satanic oppression

In 1995, in my native country, I travelled to Mossendjo, a small town located in the north-west side of the state of Niari. I was supposed to stay there for a few days and travel back to Pointe-Noire, one of the southernmost coastal cities in the country. One evening, I went to pay a visit to my late aunty, the wife of one of my late paternal uncles. She welcomed me with joy.

I sat down by the wooden fire in a small kitchen as it was a bit cold during the dry season. The fire was burning swiftly and the light in the kitchen bright. I took a wooden stool made of limba, a famous tree type used to make furniture, and sat on it. I started gazing around the kitchen. My aunty was busy arranging the messy surroundings. She knew quite well about my upbringing and the boy I was, who respected her and behaved well towards her. My aunt and my mum used to get along well, and I did not see any issue spending time with her that evening. After a brief conversation with her, she served me a dinner which was composed of beans and smoked fish – which I ate with tapioca. Tapioca is a starchy substance in the form of hard white grains, obtained from cassava and used in cooking for puddings and other dishes, locally made in the Congo and some other surrounding countries in Central Africa.

I ate the food and drank two glasses of water. Around 9 p.m., I told her that I had to go back to sleep as my trip back to Pointe-Noire was scheduled for the next morning. I woke up earlier than previously planned as I felt unwell and upset. I realized that my skin was itching all over my body with a mild sensation of burning. I wanted to be near a heater or a bushfire.

After a close look, I found tiny pimples with white heads on my face, around my waist, and all over my legs. I nevertheless went to the bus station, which was located about 1 km from my aunt's place. The bus terminal was called "Mederose bus terminal," a very memorable place we used to buy groceries almost every day when we were kids. The owner of the shopping store was a businessman from Spain.

When dad was still alive, we used to stop at Mederose to do shopping. As a kid, I was very impressed by the range of goods in the store and the variety of soft drinks on the shelves. Every time I entered Mederose, my first thought was to grab a bottle of lemonade. Lemonade was a type of sweet, well-refrigerated soft drink that was somewhat different from the lemonade in Australia. Dad knew I loved drinking lemonade, and he made sure I grabbed a bottle before exiting the supermarket. At Mederose, I caught a bus that took me to the railway station, where the next train to Pointe Noire was scheduled to arrive an hour later. I knew something was not right with my skin.

I was unaware of the source of the itch. It seemed weird and unbearable.

When I got to Pointe Noire, my health condition grew worse. Mum was still alive, and when I arrived home, I explained the story to her. She looked at my skin and noticed there were millions of pimples deep in it—it seemed very surreal. The next day, I booked an appointment to see a general practitioner (GP). The doctor gave me a prescription to begin medical treatment. After two weeks of consistent treatment, nothing worked for me. I was still sick. I went to meet my GP, who told me that my sickness was not natural but spiritual. He said, "Charles, please talk to your parents and have a family meeting about your sickness." We met and decided that I should stop the medical treatment. Mum decided that I had to be taken to a church for prayer and to seek spiritual guidance, which was done. Ten days later, the pastor who prayed for me urged me to go back to my GP for further treatment. My GP met with me and smiled at me. He gave me a skin lotion, which I applied. My health was restored. Praise God!

Australia Panel Doctor Story

To be granted an Australian Postgraduate Research Visa, my wife and I needed to make an appointment with a panel doctor for a general check-up in Kuala Lumpur, Malaysia. We got to the hospital and met with the Australian panel doctor. After a thorough check-up that day, my wife was diagnosed with cancerous symptoms. She was to have a clean slate on her medical check-up. The nurse informed my wife that she had to be sick, to which she replied that she could not be sick. The nurse asked my wife if she wanted to redo the test, as she argued that she was not sick and that something was wrong with the medical testing device. My wife came out of the nurse's room and was dissatisfied with the results.

As I was sitting in the hospital waiting room, my wife and I joined hands and prayed. We believed that God was going to change the evil medical report. My wife went back in to redo the medical test, believing that the Lord Jesus was in control. So, the results came back negative, and the dark stains that had been previously reported disappeared from her chest. God can change our lives on the spot if we just trust Him.

Healed miraculously

Once upon a time, I had severe pain in my rectal area. It was so painful that I decided to book an appointment with a general practitioner (GP) to check out what was going on in my body. I went to the clinic in my suburb to book an appointment with a GP. The doctor examined me and wrote a referral letter for me to lock in a date for surgery. I went home and prayed for divine healing. On the day I was scheduled to go into the surgery room, I had a quick pre-surgery examination. The doctor on duty was astonished that the tissues in the rectal area had retracted and appeared normal. He then concluded that there was no need for surgery.

> *Isaiah 53:5 that "by the stripes of Jesus, we are healed."*

This verse resonated more in my broken world than when it was simply read from the Bible. I had personalised God's promise. God heals our diseases in Jesus' name. There is no better place to be than in the hands of God Almighty. This is what the Bible says: "Whoever dwells in the shelter of the Most-High will rest in the shadow of the Almighty." I will say of the Lord, "He is my refuge and my fortress, my God, in whom I trust." (Psalms 91:1–2).

Preaching that changed its course

In the middle of a church service in Malaysia, as I was preaching, the Holy Spirit prompted me to interrupt the delivery of my message and change the course of the service, which I did. God said to tell the whole congregation to be ready for a money miracle. I said something that I could have avoided if it was done in the flesh or if I didn't have faith in God. I had never done this in my ministry except in that morning service.

I said, "Please bring to the pulpit all your bags or purses if you want God to do a financial miracle right now. It sounded weird, unnatural, and quite daunting. I had never prayed such a risky prayer in front of so many people in church. People started rushing to the pulpit and leaving their purses and bags. I also told them to make sure they could easily identify their purses when I finished praying. After praying, I asked the church members to take back their bags or wallets. Afterwards, the service was run as usual and ended with thanksgiving to God.

Monday was the following day, and one church member called me up and said that he went to Western Union, an international money transfer company, to send some money to Africa. After his money was transferred, the receiver called and said that she received more than what was wired by Western Union from Malaysia.

The brother heard it and was amazed that the amount of money he sent had increased. He became speechless. He thought it may have been an error in calculation made by Western Union staff. He then checked the transfer slip and said to the receiver, "This is what I sent. But the receiver further argued that when she went to the Western Union office in Cameroon, the staff found on the screen an amount that was different from what the sender put through.

The receiver thought that our church member had become insane. To simplify the matter, he told the receiver he now knew where the problem lay as he connected the dots back to the church service, we had had the day before. The sender then said, "Thank you for letting me know, and I'll talk to you later." So, the phone conversation ended on an astonishing note. Thank you very much, my brother. Can God bring money out of nowhere? Yes, he can. That was what I call a supernatural increase.

Supernatural payment of our rent in Malaysia

It is written: "God is all-knowing" (Psalm 147:5). In Malaysia, there was a month we were running late to make a bank transfer for our rent. We did not have enough cash that month. We prayed that God would provide us with some money, but nothing seemed to work. We could not get enough money in time. We started being afraid of what the landlord would say or do if the rental payment date passed without payment. After two days of languishing and waiting upon God, the landlord called me. He said, "Thank you very much, Charles, for paying your rent for this month."

Suddenly, I had goosebumps and mixed feelings of joy and doubt. I thought the landlord had become delusional or had lost his mind because the facts were contrary to the situation on the ground. I stayed silent and waited for everyone to come home in the evening. Our household included people who needed shelter and whom we took in.

We sat around the table for dinner, and I started to reflect on what really went on that day. I then broke the news to everyone, to their great amazement. We all agreed that God performed a miracle by paying our house rent, as we were financially tight. God is a miracle-worker. He can do amazing things in the nick of time.

Physical healing and heavenly drops

A cyst started growing in my right arm in 2007 and has disappeared till today. I have had no pain in my wrist since. Isn't it amazing? On the eve of Christmas in 2008, in Malaysia, we had insufficient groceries for the festive season. We prayed that God might open the windows of heaven to us. The children in the house (whom we had taken in) urged me to find some money and give it to my wife to buy some groceries. The funniest part of the story is that I agreed to do so because I knew God was going to give me some cash. Simple faith can produce extraordinary results!

Before I went to bed, I knew the pressure was mounting for me to provide for the family. I went to bed anyway with the assurance that something was about to happen. The next morning, I woke up around 6 a.m., took my shower, and went out at about 7 a.m.

While most people were still in their homes, I stepped out and began to walk down the narrow footpath in front of our residential area. I marched for approximately 100 meters, and suddenly, when I looked down, I saw two 100-Malaysian-dollar bank notes on the ground. The wind was not strong, and it could not blow banknotes far away—thank God. Mild winds are sometimes beneficial because they do not lift leaves and throw litter. I thought I was daydreaming when I saw the money on the ground right in front of me. A voice whispered in my ears, "Pick it up; it is yours." Praise God for provision.

Supernatural intervention: Hear, connect, and receive

One day in Malaysia, I was short of 1,500 USD to pay some bills, including my rent. I went to God and asked for help. He answered me like this: "Charles, you have to go to Daniel; I have commanded him to give you the 1,500 USD." I asked God for clarification about the three friends having the same name as Daniel. I said to God that I have a friend who lives in the Congo whose name is Daniel, and I have two other friends of the same name living in South Korea and Malaysia. God replied, "Go to your friend who resides in South Korea and tell him that God has sent me to you to request a financial assistance of 1500 USD."

I emailed him and waited for his reply. When I got my friend's answer, he said, "The moment I read your message, my heart was filled with compassion and peace." I now want to transfer to you the 1500 USD you requested. He then asked for my bank account details. Out of curiosity, he asked me, "Can you please explain how God directed you to me?"

I told him the whole story. After a while, he wired me USD 1500. God does speak to His children; He really cares for us in times of need.

Chapter Four

Resilience and Pursuit

The American Psychological Association defines resilience as the capacity to adapt in the face of difficulties, trauma, adversity, hardship, and tragedy (Southwick et al., 2014). As a child of God, I have discovered that it takes the Holy Spirit to enable us to stand strong in tough times. We always need God to sustain us during those trying moments. I have been in that space many times. I think many people have been in that space too.

Many factors, such as emotional, biological, psychological, social, and cultural ones, cause us to respond differently to stressful situations. But if we allow God to step in, we can surely pass through certain storms without becoming victims of them. So, when we choose to walk with God, we are not immune to storms. They come and go. God often allows storms to build up our faith and ultimately sharpen and form us the way He wants.

Determination is the ability to try something or to be firm in one's purpose. God says in Isaiah 41:10, "So do not fear, for I am with you; do not be dismayed, for I am your God." I will strengthen you and help you. "I will uphold you with my righteous right hand."

Faith-driven trip: flying off to Malaysia

In 1998, I had a dream in which I saw my late father-in-law, who told me to leave the Congo, my native country. He said to me sternly, "Charles, this is no longer your place." "You have to go away from here." I woke up and realised it was just a dream. With the political instability and the killing of civilians in the Congo in those days, my wife and I decided to leave for Malaysia in Southeast Asia.

Between 1994 and 1999, I was preparing for a trip to Malaysia to further my studies. I did my undergraduate studies in the Congo entirely in French. Congo is a former French colony, and the medium of instruction is French from kindergarten to university. I want to explain here how the whole idea of going to Malaysia came about.

I graduated with a master's degree from the Faculty of Sciences, Department of Geology, at Marien Ngouabi University in the Congo. I looked for jobs right after my graduation. However, I could not find one, and I became frustrated. While on a job search, I went to many interviews but did not land a job. In 1996, I found a job as a petroleum geologist to conduct applied research on the hydrocarbon potential of the northern Congolese sedimentary basin.

I was assigned to a team to work in the vicinity of the town of Ouesso, a cosmopolitan city in the state of Cuvette in my native country's northern region. At the time, we were still grappling with the aftermath of the civil war that dissected the nation and caused chaos across various tribal groups. I received a phone call from the head of the geology department, Dr. Kinga Mouzeo. He urged me to catch the earliest train to the capital city, Brazzaville. My sister received the call from him too and declined the idea of me joining the research team in Ouesso due to social and ethnic tensions occurring across the state. Anyway, I decided to go to Brazzaville to attend the pre-trip technical meeting.

It is often difficult to comprehend the mystery of God's care for our lives. Have you ever asked why God allowed certain things to happen in your life? After the briefing, we left for Ouesso.

In Ouesso, during my field work with my university professor, something devastating happened. The professor loved God. Every day, I saw him reading the Bible and praying. One day, he got the bad news that his wife was seriously injured in a car crash on her way to the airport for an overseas trip.

He took a break and returned to his hometown to see his family and learn the truth about what had happened. I asked the question, "Why did God allow that to happen to him?" In the same way, as you read this book, you may be facing a difficult time. I guarantee you that God is in control. Can God be in control and at the same time allow messy stuff in our lives?

Mark 4:37

"A storm battered severely against the boat where Jesus and His disciples were".

Often, when hit by a storm, we think that God has abandoned us or is far away. In addition, the fact that God is not physically present makes us feel vulnerable, as if God has not shown concern for our trials. The Bible says in the book of Genesis that the Egyptians forced the Israelites to labour for nearly 430 years (e.g., Exodus 2: 25). And Pharaoh, the king of Egypt at the time, feared the growing presence of the Israelites. The Israelites were in limbo and could not find a way out of their enslavement. God waited for His own timing to mightily act and deliver the Israelites out of slavery. The psalmist said that God is a refuge for the oppressed, a refuge in times of trouble (Psalm 9:9). It means that, regardless of the nature of your problem, God is still present right where you are.

God does care every step of the way

When my wife and I were planning to go to Malaysia to take up a placement at a university, we did not have financial support from family members or from the Congolese government. We were working and saved some money to just purchase our airline tickets.

We didn't have enough money to buy a ticket for our daughter or to have a safety net while in Kuala Lumpur, Malaysia. We ended up saving USD 210 as a cash reserve prior to leaving for Malaysia. Planning for the Malaysian trip sounded like a free fall into an abyss!

God gave us the courage to move on and stick to our plans. Faith works when you do not focus on the smallness of what you have but rather on how big God is. We took a flight from the city of Pointe Noire and headed south to Angola, where we had a stopover. We landed in South Africa the same day.

What was it like to touch down at Johannesburg Airport? We had no place to stay overnight at the airport. We were waiting for a connecting flight with Malaysia Airlines to get to Kuala Lumpur the next day. That was the first time I set foot outside of the Congo.

While we were stranded at the airport, we met a brother in Christ who came to Johannesburg to pick up his daughter. Coincidentally, that brother was living in Kuala Lumpur, the city to which we were bound to travel the following day. He asked us if we had a place to stay at the airport; we told him that we planned to stay overnight on the passenger chairs.

He went and booked a master room, fully paid, in one of the five-star hotels so that we could spend a night there. The next day, we flew to Malaysia. On arrival, we were provided with our first accommodation at a cozy apartment on the 14th floor of the Pantai Tower in Kuala Lumpur, Malaysia. We stayed at this luxurious apartment for two weeks. We were close to ending our stay at this apartment when the owner told us to vacate without paying. We could not expect that in a foreign land. That was amazing - God did it for us.

Our second accommodation was at the home of Dr. Paramanathan, also known as Dr. Param. We stayed at his house free of charge. We used power and the telephone to make local calls without contributing to any bills.

Our third accommodation was at Brother Samuel Jones' university apartment. Brother Samuel Jones was approached by Professor Lee Chai Peng. We did not know of the initial arrangements made by Professor Lee Chai Peng, looking for a place for us to stay. I learned that when you are lamenting

Chapter Four: Resilience and Pursuit

about a problem, God can make some people uncomfortable until they get something fixed for you.

When we had nothing to pay for my university tuition fees, God touched the heart of Dr. Paramanathan, who signed a check for RM5, 000 which was not a loan but a gift. That was mind-blowing, given the circumstances in which we were.

Confirmation of the call of God

I always wanted to pursue theological studies, but I did not have the financial means to do it. How did it all happen? After four months of postgraduate education at the University of Malaya pursuing my Master of Geoscience, a professor of geology in the department had a chat with me. He is a Christian and a strong believer. One day, he said, "Charles, I have something to tell you." Can we have time to discuss and find common ground?

I went to see him in the late hours of one morning. I sat down in front of him, and he looked at me with his crystal-clear spectacles like a general practitioner observing his patient. He said, "Charles, I heard from God telling me you have not come to Malaysia to just study geology." You have a call of God upon your life. He said his church management was willing to sponsor my theological studies. As I paused, I was instantly chilled by his words.

He told me to think things over for a while and return to him after I had decided. That evening, I got on my knees, and God spoke to me, saying I sent my son Lee to you. God wanted me to make room for what he was up to. For me, that was a confirmation of the call of God on me. I went to meet

Professor Lee and unpacked what I treasured in my heart. I frankly said that God put in my heart the desire to take leave from my Master of Science programme and dedicate quality time to my theological training.

We then agreed that I would go full-time at the Bible College and enroll at the School of Acts in Malaysia. One morning, we rode on Prof. Lee's motorbike to meet the principal of the school, Rev. Raymond Mooi. We had a meeting and discussed my enrolment in detail. Professor Lee Chai Peng said that the school fees would be paid by the church where he was the Treasurer, and on top of that, I would receive a living allowance for food, transportation, and electricity bills. Praise God and his unlimited resources.

As I learned here, the call of God cannot be faked: "You are either called by God or you call yourself." There is no half-measure in fulfilling our destiny in God. The true call of God comes with confirmation. The theological training was an eye-opener. I graduated from the School of Acts, Class of 2000. I then returned to the University of Malaya to complete my master's degree in geoscience. As I prayed about the need to do further theological studies, God urged a brother in the Lord to sponsor my studies at a Malaysian Mission School. In the middle of my master's program, I got some funding to do a diploma in cross-cultural studies at the Malaysian Centre for Global Ministry (MCGM).

Scholarship awarded for MSc and PhD programs

I was the winner of two scholarships totaling over 200,000 Australian dollars to undertake master's and PhD degrees at the University of Tasmania. The scholarships covered tuition fees, laboratory fees, and accommodation. Such a gift from God is unfathomable, as I come from a middle-class family. The idea of attending world-class universities had never crossed my mind when I was in the Congo. God still does miracles!

I recalled writing to the University of Adelaide (Australia) in 1996 with the intent of pursuing my postgraduate studies in geology. The Registrar replied to my request, and the tuition fee figure was so high at that time that I concluded I would never study at an Australian university. Guess what! Never give up until God has his final say. If someone is alive, there is still hope. With God, you can make a way in the wilderness. There is light at the end of the tunnel. The truth is that God never stops working even when we don't see Him.

CHAPTER FIVE
DIVINE PROTECTION

The way I was brought up gave me the assurance that God protects his children from harm. He's always been by my side, no matter where I go. He is a caring father who makes certain that His children are safe and enjoy life.

My toddler's experience

I was literally saved at the age of three from drowning in a water-filled bucket. I learned that God works in the background when you don't even notice. What God does is incomprehensible. Sometimes, the little things God does are commonly overlooked. In fact, God does many little things that are significant in His eyes, yet we are not aware of His hand in them. This is a true story narrated by my late sister in 2014. My sister disclosed what occurred 44 years ago.

One day, as I was preparing a church seminar while on holiday at a local church in the Congo, I was not aware that my sister had been ministered to by the Holy Spirit a day before; she narrated, "I sat at the edge of my bed and God began to talk to me last night." I could not sleep and started recalling the event afresh, as on day one. And God told me to break the silence about the act of saving the life of my younger brother Charles more than 44 years ago.

On the day I was scheduled to minister, my sister asked the lead pastor to give her a time slot for testimony. She stood up on the stage and paused a few times before narrating the ordeal. I had a feeling she was going to say something delightful about me as I sat in the front row during the church service. I started listening intently while gazing at her eyes.

She commenced by saying, "People of God, I have something important to disclose that relates to my younger brother, Pastor Charles, who is sitting in the front row." Suddenly, I felt a kick in my stomach, as if I had digestive problems. I took control over the disturbance and behaved as if I did not hear anything from her. She went on saying, "When my younger brother was still crawling (about 2-years-old) during his childhood days, he narrowly missed death." I was plaiting my friend's hair, and there was a bucket filled with water sitting some meters away from where we were. I took my eyes off Charles when he went close to the bucket.

I thought everything looked normal and kept my eyes on my friend's head. After a moment, a man came running towards my little brother. The unknown man quickly ran, caught the child, and lifted him out of the bucket filled with water. I turned and saw the child crying, and he almost passed out. While panicking, I looked out and saw that the man had left the child with me. I took my little brother in my hands and shook him up to bring him back to his senses. Thank God he came back and regained consciousness. My sister's lessons from that lived experienced are the following – and she said:

1) God knew my little brother since he was in our mother's womb (Jeremiah 5:1).
2) God saved my little brother because He knew that he had not started his mission on earth yet. God's eyes were on my little brother even when no one knew his whereabouts when that incident occurred. God sent an angel to rescue by brother. Seeing my brother serving God as a Pastor is not mere coincidence. He was truly called by God.
3) God had assigned an angel for a specific mission. Lifting my little brother was a clear indication of God's protection.
4) God is very protective. He did that to Jesus Christ His only son to save Him from the hands of Romans by sending Him over to Egypt until the death of Herod.

Hidden in the shelter of God's wings

Psalm 91:1

"He who dwells in the shelter of the Most-High will rest in the shadow of the Almighty."

I will say of the LORD, "He is my refuge and my fortress, my God, in whom I trust." I have been enjoying God's protection since I was born. But it does not mean I have been immune to satanic oppression or attacks. The fact is, we live in a fallen world where things might take some bad turns that may potentially damage our self-image. People have literally said things that are untrue about my life, which is hurting, and such accusations are signs of evil machination.

God's faithfulness – my anchor

Do we all know the 233 code of Heaven?

> *The answer is 2 Thessalonians 3:3. This verse says, "But the Lord is faithful, and He will strengthen you and protect you from the evil one."*

I can say to everyone that there is a God who is the Creator of this universe. He is faithful. While everything around us may fall apart, God can cause us to bounce back and go extra miles in life. I am a living testimony of God's faithfulness. He never leaves us, even at the edge of a cliff. If God wants you to go down the "Abyss", He may allow it for a purpose, but He will travel with you to the very end.

God is my strength every step of the way

> *Psalm 46:1*
>
> *God is our refuge and strength, an ever-present help in trouble.*

God is our PLACE OF SAFETY. There were many times in my life I felt like giving up, but God came in at the last minute and opened new horizons and opportunities in my life. I am typing these words to say with all my strength that God is there for you in your most difficult times. He is right there with you—by your bedside at the hospital, in the confinement of your prison cell, and even in your lonely place.

Sudden arrest by militia– an unforgettable experience

During the 1994 cease-fire ordered by both the government and the opposition party in the Republic of the Congo, I was suddenly arrested. The capital city of Congo, Brazzaville, was quiet and lifeless; all supermarkets were closed, streets were deserted, and the University Marien Ngouabi, where I studied, was also closed, and students took most of their lectures in an irregular manner. The community was all scared by the daily crackling of gunshots and military vehicles patrolling the streets. We could see the marks of bullets on the walls of the house every time we woke up. What was even more scary and surreal was when we heard people fighting across the street or on the driveway.

I had a dream in which some people and I were arrested by gunmen. In the morning, my friend and I wanted to have some time out. We did so and were later captured by a group of armed men. How did that happen?

There was intense shelling in the neighborhood, and many bullets hit my house as well that week. During that week, I felt that something was not right. I wanted to change my mind and tell my friend to defer our time out or at least to go to another suburb on another occasion. My friend insisted and came and picked me up on his motorcycle. We set out for

Chapter Five: Divine Protection

another part of the city. He drove for about 30 minutes away from my house. We rode into a militia ambush, which seemed to be a stronghold for gunmen and their accomplices.

We saw a man with a blood-sucking face who looked like a zombie and who did not talk much. He was glad to see two young men, whom he called intruders. He said proudly that he had not seen the blood of any human being since the day began. The scene was so hostile that we were convinced it was going to be our last day to be alive. That was a traumatising experience that I had never experienced.

The man took a rifle and loaded bullets. He was so furious; we were sure he wanted us killed. He told us that if we disobeyed his orders, he would pull the trigger at any time. I visualised what Heaven would look like if we were to be killed at that moment. Although it was 2:30 p.m. that day, the sky became black for me. This reminded me that the Bible says the sky blackened prior to my Lord and Savior Jesus Christ giving his last breath.

I had the unusual experience of doing a quick "mental tour" of my entire family. I thought about my mum and others. I said silently, "Mum, I love you, and we shall certainly meet one day." I said goodbye to my two sisters. I also noted that when you are about to die, your brain is programmed differently. Your whole emotional being relocates itself and gets into a state of standstill where we often say, "I am done with this world." I felt a sense of readiness to leave this world.

Although it was emotionally painful to know that I was going to die soon, at the same time I felt a strong sense of peace knowing that I was going to meet my Lord, Jesus Christ. I became very aware of the transition from a place called Earth to a new place called Heaven. I remembered having a small blue Bible in my pocket. And I prayed a prayer of confession to God. I begged God to forgive me because He had warned me in a dream the night before that I would be arrested if I went out, and yet I did. For me, I was not determined to follow God's instructions. I knew what was going to happen to me was entirely my fault.

So, the gunman instructed us to walk in front of him, keeping a 2-meter distance between us. We walked a short distance of about 100 m, and it seemed like a never-ending walk. We felt like we took a year to complete the 100-meter walk. Then the gunman said it was time that we leave the main road and walk along a narrow footpath that was leading into the bush and close to a stream. As we were about to go down the path, an elderly man, probably in his seventies, came out of a building. What was astonishing was that he came out barefoot. It suggested that he had rushed out and seen us being taken to an unknown place.

The elderly man authoritatively stopped the gunman and asked him what was going on with us. He had him move a short distance from us and began to whisper in the gunman's ears. My friend and I were totally shocked and did not communicate during the whole ordeal. After about 10 minutes of the elderly man and the gunman's discussion, the gunman came back and told us that we were lucky. We were then released. Today, as I narrate this story, I still deeply thank God for saving me from the grips of those evil hands.

Chapter Five: Divine Protection

Holiday in Mbinda in 1978

Mbinda is a city located in the northwest of the state of Niari, in the Congo. In those days, there were many inhabitants who used to work for the mining company named Comilog. Comilog was a renowned manganese mining company. There was a cable car that transported manganese ore into Mbinda. The ore was being shipped from Gabon, transiting by railroad to Pointe-Noire Harbor before being shipped overseas. My sister, Josephine, was married to a Comilog staff member. My brother-in-law was a kind man and wanted me to do well in my studies. I went to their place for an enjoyable holiday.

At the end of my holiday, my sister bought a lot of school items, such as books, notebooks, pens, and pencils. This was the first time I had visited my sister at her marital home. We used to celebrate one of the family members' birthdays when I was a teenager. It happened that I drank two glasses of an alcoholic drink branded "Gin Tonic." The drink was sweet on my tongue. As I finished drinking, my eyes began to spin, and I felt the ground shaking. I ran into the bathroom and spent the whole night there because of the coolness inside the bathroom. As I look back, I just realise that it was God's protection that kept me alive, and no harm befell me.

Evil occurrence in my car

I once owned a Hyundai car in Malaysia. One morning, I started the car and heard the meowing sound of a cat in the engine of my car. By faith, I heard the Lord say to me, "Fear not." You can go where you want to go. My wife and I were in the car together and prayed that the cat noise would cease. The noise went on for a while and then stopped. I thought the cat had died because there was no more of the weird noise of a cat. We went to a car wash station to verify, by flushing hot water beneath my car, if a cat could be found. Nothing worked because there was no cat present, and there was no animal blood dripping from the engine parts. Unbelievable!

We concluded that it was an invisible cat. We prayed to God that such an event would not happen again. And from that day on until we disposed of the car, we had not experienced a similar strange phenomenon.

No plot against you will prevail

As an exploration geologist, I used to travel a lot in Malaysia. Once, we were in the countryside and driving on a hilly road when our 4WD pick-up Hilux skidded off the road. As that went on, the driver got injured, and the passenger with no seatbelt fastened was projected from the back seat to the dashboard. I called on the name of Jesus, and suddenly, the car not only stopped but slid to the left side of the road. This passenger was injured and started bleeding. I did not even have a bruise. I was completely injury-free. Praise God!

The whole scenario could have been deadly if it had drifted further to the right. There was a steep slope on the right side of the road. The Bible says in Romans 10:13, "Call on the name of the Lord, and you will be saved." Jesus saved me and my workmates.

Chapter Five: Divine Protection

Most horrible night ever

In 1987, on that night, I was staying in a house we were renting. That house was haunted, and I had an encounter with two spirits of the dead. As far as my recollection goes, this was the scariest experience that has occurred in my life. I was sharing the house with my late mother and nephew. One night, my mother told me that I should sleep alone in the house that night as she had to go to another suburb for a compassionate visit.

There was a person who died in the community. Mum wanted to assist and encourage the mourning family to be strong during that trying time. She thought of going out to where the funerals were being held. Strangely, I had a feeling that the approaching night was not going to be as peaceful as it used to be. However, I had no option but to spend the night alone. I was about sixteen years old. As the hours passed, I felt insecure, and my heart started racing, so something was not right deep within myself. It was the fear of the unknown that flooded my mind.

I was in a dilemma: could I leave the house and knock on the door of our neighbours at midnight? I was in a state of confusion or chaos. So, I made up my mind to stay awake until about 2am. When the time got to around 2:30 a.m., I heard a loud sound from the fence. The fence was made of aluminium sheets tied up on wooden pegs. After a few minutes, I heard two people enter the house. I was in a state of panic and started trembling in my bedroom as if electrified.

I was conscious of what was going on in the house. I asked the spirits, "Who are you?" And then one of them reacted with an incomprehensible "Hmmm." The two exchanged some words in another tribal language, which I could not understand. "Jesus, Jesus, Jesus, save me!" I yelled. I sensed that one of them was surprised to have found me in the house at that time of the night. I continued to command them to leave in a loud voice.

My lesson here was that even the spirits of the dead know the name of Jesus. I believed Jesus came and chased them out of the place. After about two hours, I came to my senses and felt relieved but exhausted until dawn. The next morning, my mother was informed by our neighbours of my ordeal fighting with two spirits of the dead. Early in the morning, I was taken by a neighbour to a church for urgent prayers.

At the church, we found a spiritual leader who looked at me and, led by the spirit of God, said, "I see that the young man Charles had a bad encounter with two spirits of the dead, and Charles had the backing of God." That's the reason the spirits of the dead could not do anything bad to me. He prayed for God's protection over me. I got lesions on my throat as a result of my shouting at the demons that night.

In Africa, we believe in witchcraft and that spirits can make noise or even travel from one place to another. We also believe that there are rebellious spirits that can harm a person. So, for me, God and his army were there to spare my life from that uncommon encounter.

My wife got bitten by a scorpion

This is one of the unusual experiences we had when residing in Malaysia. One morning, my wife got bitten by a black scorpion-looking insect. It was scary because such insects are deadly. One fact is that we were living on the 14th floor of a condominium. It was unthinkable to see an insect of that type on the 14th floor of a building. She was caught by surprise when an insect resembling a scorpion bit her. She was astonished to see the insect mark on her skin after the ordeal.

She calmly grabbed and killed the insect, then set it on a frypan and burned it. While all this scenario was going on, she gave me a call, and we prayed over it. I told her to be still because God had control over the situation. I put my trust in God, knowing that He could protect my wife. The night came, and I did not hear any bad news from her. And the next day came! I was happy and knew that the Almighty God had taken full control of the weird situation we encountered as a family. The Bible says in Luke 10:19, "I have given you authority to trample on snakes and scorpions and to overcome all the power of the enemy; nothing will harm you." We claimed this verse over my wife's life, and God intervened. He has been prolonging my wife's life ever since.

At times, we get caught in uncontrollable situations. But, during all that, God always has his eyes on us. When you stop believing in God, you give the enemy control over your destiny. There is no doubt: God carries us in his right hand. God protects His children in the midst of danger. God doesn't say we shall live in the danger-free world; however, He does promise His help whenever we are in danger.

Below are some scriptures that remind us of God's protection and care.

Psalm 91: 1-7 [NIV]

¹ Whoever dwells in the shelter
   of the Most High
   will rest in the shadow of the Almighty.
² I will say of the Lord, "He is my
   refuge and my fortress,
   my God, in whom I trust."
³ Surely he will save you
   from the fowler's snare
   and from the deadly pestilence.
⁴ He will cover you with his feathers,
   and under his wings you will find refuge;
   his faithfulness will be your
   shield and rampart.
⁵ You will not fear the terror of night,
   nor the arrow that flies by day,
⁶ nor the pestilence that stalks
   in the darkness,
   nor the plague that destroys at midday.
⁷ A thousand may fall at your side,
   ten thousand at your right hand,
   but it will not come near you.

Psalm 34: 7 [Amplified Bible]

The angel of the Lord encamps around those who fear Him, and He delivers them.

Chapter Five: Divine Protection

2 Thessalonians 3: 3 *[Amplified Bible]*

But the Lord is faithful, and He will strengthen you and protect you from the evil one.

Psalm 17: 8-9 *[Amplified Bible]*

Keep me [in Your affectionate care, protect me] as the apple of Your eye.
Hide me in the [protective] shadow of Your wings
From the wicked who despoil and deal violently with me,
My deadly enemies who surround me.

Deuteronomy 31: 6 *[Amplified Bible]*

Be strong and courageous, do not be afraid or tremble in dread before them, for it is the Lord your God who goes with you. He will not fail you or abandon you.

The Bible says Christ has "disarmed the rulers and authorities" and "made a public display of them" (Colossians 2:15). Christians need to take seriously the fact that Jesus has given them power and authority over evil spiritual powers. (Luke 9:1; Matthew 28:20).

Chapter Six
Divine Guidance

Several times, I have been enticed to accept ungodly advice that could have shortened my life. When I was 10 years old, a cousin told me to follow him to a nearby river and get washed by him. He said I would become intelligent and excel in my studies if I heeded his counsel. At that time, I was in primary school. To further entice me to accept his views, he recounted to me how successful he was, as witnessed by his giving me clothes and delicious food and drinks.

He used to bring his girlfriend to where I was staying and used to say, "Charles, you will get many blessings if you follow in my footsteps." One day, he asked me to follow him to a river about a mile away from our residential area. I found it very suspicious and went to talk to my mum. I explained everything to my mother, and she told me not to follow my cousin's evil plans, which I thankfully did not. She said he must be a witch.

When I was 28 years old, a maternal uncle asked me for my consent if he could do some magic and help me find a highly paid job, a few years after I completed my master's degree in the Congo. I told him that I would give it a second thought. I soon realised that it was a stratagem set up against me for my uncle's own selfish ambitions and a craving desire to fulfil his evil plans to make my life miserable.

The gathering of angels

I had travelled 75 kilometres on a highway from Kuala Lumpur, Malaysia's capital city, at this point on my road trip. I heard God say to me, "Slow down, Charles." Without second-guessing, I heeded the voice and started to reduce speed from approximately 100 km/h to about 50 km/h. Suddenly, my car started to veer off the road, which was followed by a loud sound of bursting on the right side of my car. The front right tyre had burst, and the car became difficult to control. I was only able to control the car because I was no longer moving at such a high speed. Fortunately, there was no car behind me—thank God! I safely pulled over and stopped the car.

As I was doing it alone, it took me some time to replace the damaged tyre with my spare tyre. I got back on the road and arrived safely at my workplace, although late. To God be the glory for having saved my life from death. But I also know that if God permitted death, I would have gone to Heaven to be with Him forever.

Leaning on God

Contrary to what I narrated in Chapter 4 about my theological education, I bring here a different account of when man proposes, and God disposes. I wanted to go to Europe to pursue postgraduate studies in geology, but things did not work out the way I planned. In early January 2000, I arrived in Malaysia to do a Master of Science in clastic sedimentology at the top Malaysian university, called the University of Malaya.

I started the course, and at some point, I began to experience some financial difficulties. It was God who was planning a different thing in my life. God spoke to one of my research advisors, Professor Lee Chai Peng. One morning, he called me into his office for a tête-à-tête. He said, "Charles, I have been visited by God about you." That baffled me. He then told me.

"God said to me that you did not come to Malaysia to only read geology." You have another task that God wants you to embark on. God has a different plan for you when you leave Malaysia. I did not want him to use the words "leave Malaysia." It was surprising that he heard from God about me. Relating to my story, God does speak to us through people who are around us or even not connected to us. But we sometimes harden our hearts, and the opportunity may slip away. So, what God intends for us can be redirected to another human being whose heart is soft.

I asked him to tell me in detail what God had said to him. Prof. Lee urged me to take a Certificate in Ministry Training at the School of Acts or continue with my Masters in Geology. He also added that the Certificate in Ministry Training would be fully funded if I wanted to do a theology course. I went home sad and wondered why I should stop studying. I shared Professor Lee's thoughts with my wife, and we prayed about it. I took the matter to God, as I knew the heavy load that was on my shoulders. I needed God to directly speak to me.

Within the same week, I got a prompt from God that I should enroll in the theological course. To do that, I had to write a letter to my supervisor stating that I needed some time off or a break to do Bible studies. Now, the most intriguing part of all was that my supervisor was a Muslim. I became concerned about what would happen if he denied my request. I prayed that God would touch his heart and that I would be granted six months of research leave. My supervisor took a deep breath and said that what you are asking has never been requested. He asked me a funny question: "Are you going to be a father?" In other words, was I going to be a priest?

I smiled and responded that, God willing, I might be a priest. And he said, "Okay." He also said, "I will approve your request," which he did. It reassured me that God answers our prayers beyond what we can ask or imagine. He is a miracle worker, the God of the impossible.

Flashbacks

I remember when I was in the Congo. I used to dream about a constant vision of holding a big book in my hands. The book resembles a huge encyclopedia, which I thought was God's way of telling me to deepen my knowledge of His Word. I did not know how God was going to unwrap His plans in my life. I began to connect the dots when I was pondering Professor Lee's approach. The next morning, I got an answer from God, which I held. The impression I was getting was that my wife was not going to welcome my decision to put a stop to my graduate studies for a period of six months. In the end, she was supportive.

Once upon a time, I had plan A, but God had plan B. I first planned to do my doctoral degree in geology at the

University of Malaya in Malaysia in petroleum systems so that I might work in the oil and gas industry. That was my dream, and I assumed I had received God's approval. After continued prayers, I went ahead and submitted a doctoral research proposal. To be honest, I did not get clear guidance from God. I was very much guided by my emotions rather than the Holy Spirit. Later, God changed the whole plan and led me to the University of Tasmania in Australia.

Elisabeth Elliott, a Christian author, and speaker, once said, "We have ample evidence that the Lord can guide because His promises cover every imaginable situation." "All we have to do is take His (God's) hand."
Using the case of the prophet Elijah in 1 Kings 17, we vividly discover the way God directed the steps of Elijah after a severe drought in his hometown of Tishbite. Elijah announced the drought. Elijah the Tishbite, from Tishbe in Gilead, now told King Ahab, "As the Lord, the God of Israel, lives, whom I serve, and there will be no dew or rain in the next few years except at my word," Elijah was a man of faith. When he declared the drought before the king, God gave him full support.

As a child of God, we must be careful when declaring things. For example, one day, I was vexed by something that happened in my ministry. Without going into detail, I said to those opposing me, "If I am called by God, something will happen before the month of June." Regrettably, I must state that something bad did occur. I found out that when a child of God is hurt, he or she should not wish evil on his attackers because God could strike them with His anger. God told me, "Don't do that in the future." "I was hurt when you were hurt," God said.

God took me to the story of Elisha when he cursed the young men in 2 Kings 2:23–25. It reads "23." From there, Elisha went up to Bethel. As he was walking along the road, some boys came out of the town and jeered at him. "Get out of here, Baldy!" they said. "Get out of here, baldy!" 24 He turned around, looked at them, and called down a curse on them in the name of the Lord. Then two bears came out of the woods and mauled forty-two of the boys. 25 And he went on to Mount Carmel, and from there he returned to Samaria.

God told me that when we are hurt, we have two options: compassion or vengeance. God said my son, Jesus Christ, never reacted when hurt with a heart to return evil for evil. God took me to the cross and said, "Please read Luke 23:34." I read the verse, and clearly Jesus was the only human being, fully divine and fully human, who had the most compassionate heart. While Jesus was experiencing the most humiliating death humanity has ever seen, he said, "Father, forgive them, for they do not know what they are doing." And they divided up his clothes by casting lots. God calls us to look at the cross every day, reflecting on the finished work of redemption. Simply put, in the Old Testament and the New Testament, God says revenge is His. Romans 12:19; Leviticus 19:18; and Proverbs 24:29

Elijah fed by ravens: An unusual food supply

1 Kings 17: 2-10

Verse 2. Then the word of the Lord came to Elijah: verse 3: "Leave here, turn eastward, and hide in the Kerith Ravine, east of the Jordan." Verse 4: "You will drink from the brook, and I have directed the ravens to supply you with food there." Verse 5. So, he did what the Lord had told him. He went to the Kerith Ravine, east of the Jordan, and stayed there. Verse 7. Sometime later, the brook dried up because there had been no rain on the land. 8. Then the word of the Lord came to him: Verse 9. "Go at once to Zarephath in the region of Sidon and stay there." I have directed a widow there to supply you with food.

Verse 10. So, he went to Zarephath. When he came to the town gate, a widow was there gathering sticks. He called to her and asked, "Would you bring me a little water in a jar so I may have a drink?"

In the three first verses, we realise that God became more concerned about Elijah's conditions. God knew that Elijah was not comfortable in his own skin. God always steps in when we expect it the least. I asked the question of why God had to urge Elijah to leave in verse 3. God could have blessed him right there, but he chose to bring a raven to Elijah in another location.

God revealed to me that the place Elijah went to hide or run from Jezebel was not the place of his further assignment. God had not finished with Elijah yet, and He prompted him to travel east of the Jordan. Out of obedience, Elijah departed and arrived at the Kerith Ravine. Acts of obedience always bring down heavenly blessings.

If God can use a bird to feed a human being, He will use human beings to assist other human beings. The Parable of the Good Samaritan is an excellent example of a human helping another human in despair.

Key No. 1: obedience

Before Elijah left Tishbite, he made a prophetic declaration of no rain in the land, which happened. Prior to meeting the widow at Zarephath, God was already working in the background to prepare that widow. God said to Elijah, "Go to Zarephath, there is a woman there who will give you food."

Abram obeyed God, and a ram was provided by God to be a substitute for his son Isaac to carry out the sacrifice. Elijah knew that the will of God was to leave Tishbite and move to Zarephath. We need to spend quality time reading and memorising God's word (logos) and let him speak to us by giving us the rhema word (revelation). The Fall in the Garden of Eden (Genesis 3) was the result of disobedience.

Zarephath was the God-chosen location. For example, if God did not call you to nightclub evangelism, then don't try it.

Key No. 2: Generosity and Hospitality

When Elijah got to the town gate, he saw a widow who was piling up sticks. She was doing her routine work to be resourceful and look after her household. She had no husband, which put some burden on her to make ends meet. At this point, I realised that the widow had spiritual, emotional, and financial needs.

I remember how my late dad used to give clothes to people. He used to ask my late mother to give away some of her unworn (not damaged or shabby looking) clothes to women, and he promised to buy new ones for her. Dad taught me a lesson: we should help those in need. The way we plan our lives today will have important implications not only for our own lives but also for the lives of our children, grandchildren, and great-grandchildren. Elijah said to the widow, "Bring me some water in a jar," which she did.

> *Luke 6:38 says, "Give, and it will be given to you." A good measure, pressed down, shaken together, and running over, will be poured into your lap. "Because the measure you use will be measured to you." If you give away money, it might not come back to you in the form of money, but it might be healing or something else.*
>
> *Matthew 25:35 Jesus said to his disciples, "For I was hungry, and you gave me something to eat; I was thirsty, and you gave me something to drink; I was a stranger, and you invited me in."*

Back home, in 1999, we used to have lunch with an autistic church member. He had some sort of brain disorder. Here, I am not trying to single him out because of his illness, but I am using this example to show that we did not behave indifferently towards that brother. My wife and I knew that every person has worth in the eyes of God. So, there was no point in not welcoming that brother to our house for lunch.

1 Kings 17: 11-12

Verse 11. As she was going to get it, he called, "And bring me, please, a piece of bread."

Verse 12. "As surely as the Lord your God lives," she replied, "I don't have any bread—only a handful of flour in a jar and a little olive oil in a jug. I am gathering a few sticks to take home and make a meal for myself and my son that we may eat it and die."

Key No. 3: Anxiety is something to avoid

The widow became worried because Elijah had gone too far by asking her to bring him a piece of bread. The question here is, "Do we always cast our cares upon the Lord?" Well, we often take matters into our own hands.

She felt she was running low as the small portion of flour and olive oil would soon be consumed. We often react differently to changing circumstances in our lives. The question is: How do we behave when the clock is ticking on low income, worsening health conditions, or even awaiting the outcome of a job application?

1 Kings 17: 13

> *Verse 13. Elijah said to her, "Don't be afraid." Go home and do as you have said. But first, make a small loaf of bread for me from what you have and bring it to me, and then make something for yourself and your son.*

Key No. 4: Fear not

Some of the fears that may hold us back from planning our lives are:

Fear of change and fear of loneliness.

Fear of rejection and failure.

Fear of uncertainty and running out of resources (for example, the widow of Zarephath).

Fear of being judged and being inadequate (inadequacy).

Fear of doom (that something bad will happen).

To be honest, people will not be driving on the road if the fear of doom is in their mind.

Chapter Six: Divine Guidance

Key No. 5: Godly counsel unlocks the treasures of Heaven

1 Kings 17: 14-16

14) For this is what the Lord, the God of Israel, says: "The jar of flour will not be used up, and the jug of oil will not run dry until the day the Lord sends rain on the land."

15) She went away and did as Elijah had told her. So, there was food every day for Elijah and for the woman and her family.

16) For the jar of flour was not used up and the jug of oil did not run dry, in keeping with the word of the Lord spoken by Elijah.

Genesis 17: 15-18

Verse 15. God also said to Abraham, "As for Sarai your wife, you are no longer to call her Sarai; her name will be Sarah. Verse 16. I will bless her and will surely give you a son by her. I will bless her so that she will be the mother of nations; kings of peoples will come from her."

Verse 17. Abraham fell facedown; he laughed and said to himself, "Will a son be born to a man a hundred years old? Will Sarah bear a child at the age of ninety?" Verse 18. And Abraham said to God, "If only Ishmael might live under your blessing!".

Genesis 21: 1-6

Verse 1. Now the LORD was gracious to Sarah as he had said, and the LORD did for Sarah what he had promised. Verse ² Sarah became pregnant and bore a son to Abraham in his old age, at the very time God had promised him. Verse ³ Abraham gave the name Isaac[a] to the son Sarah bore him. Verse ⁴ When his son Isaac was eight days old, Abraham circumcised him, as God commanded him. Verse ⁵ Abraham was a hundred years old when his son Isaac was born to him.

Verse ⁶ Sarah said, "God has brought me laughter, and everyone who hears about this will laugh with me."

God guides us by following His will—that's the bottom line in divine guidance. One of the most challenging spiritual exercises that Christians will ever undertake is obeying God's will. In John 4:34, "My food," said Jesus, "is to do the will of him who sent me and to finish his work." It is also said in Luke 22:42. "Father, if you are willing, take this cup from me; yet not my will, but yours be done."

Jesus set a good example of an unwavering pursuit of His Father's will amid suffering and misery. Jesus Christ is our great example, which we should follow at all costs. It is hard to follow God's will when we are shattered by the challenges of life. I used to believe that God's will was for everything to work perfectly as I imagined it. With a long list of wants, not always needs, I often anticipate success in all I do, but it turns out to be different in the end. I have had several achievements;

however, I have not succeeded in all my attempts. I have learned that we learn to live in God's will as we continue to grow in Him. In fact, challenges are all part of the process of growing in Him.

For example, there came a time when I was planning to travel to London, UK, for a pastoral internship right after my graduation from a Bible seminary in Malaysia. Most travel arrangements were made, and we were waiting for the outcome of a missionary family visa to leave for the United Kingdom.

Knowing that God was about to change our story made me happy. After nearly six months, my wife and I were saddened by the negative outcome of the visa application. In that very season, the United Kingdom had put some restrictions on missionary visas, and we had to wait until further notice. The news brought tears of despair to our eyes, and we needed to overcome the pain.

We became literally helpless and wanted to go to Thailand and live on the island of Phuket. A few months later, the island was hit by a tsunami, which made us change our minds and plan differently. Destruction of the land was widespread, and many people lost their lives. We said to ourselves that it was God's plan to forbid us from travelling to Phuket.

In the book of Isaiah, the Bible says, "My thoughts are not yours, says God." Abram was disappointed after trying to solve matters with his strength and custom-bound principles. We should not do things in a customary way. Do not follow the crowd, follow godly principles. God is not controlled by our customs or traditions. He is all-powerful, and he can rule out or bring in all that is needed to implement what God finds best in His eyes.

> *The Bible says in Luke 1:37, "For nothing is impossible with God." (New International Version): "For no word from God shall be void of power." (American Standard Version); "For no promise from God will be impossible of fulfillment" (Weymouth New Testament Version); "With God nothing shall be impossible." King James Version (Cambridge Edition). I have listed a few Bible verses to express with clarity how God can turn our situations around.*

Today, the Holy Spirit has spoken to me to encourage us, as the days we are living are evil and the devil still roars like a lion looking for someone to devour. As you are reading, victory will locate you in your world, and the gates of disappointment and shame will tumble. You may be facing a mountain where you say that God has left you, or He may be far away. God is about to surprise you! The thunder of God's promises will shake up your wilderness, blow into pieces the blocks of your defeats, and scatter the obstacles of things against you.

Let's look at the beginning

> ### *Genesis 1:1-2*
>
> *__1__ In the beginning God created the heaven and the earth.*
> *__2__ And the earth was without form, and void; and darkness was upon the face of the deep.*

Chapter Six: Divine Guidance

And the Spirit of God moved upon the face of the waters.

The earth had no form, and God breathed His breath to orchestrate the mechanism of creation in the emptiness of the deep. When God spoke, things began to happen. For it is certain that God has the power to create. He operates in the realm of emptiness and brings into existence what we have not seen in the natural realm.

In Genesis 1:2, God spoke, "Let there be light, and there was light." No word from God is powerless.

Every divine word is purposeful. There may be something troubling you, and you don't even know when your next breakthrough might happen or even how it might occur. Believe God's word; he shall transform your world. You are at the edge of something bigger that is going to tingle the eyes of passersby. As God demonstrated His power to Abram, so it will be in our lives.

Genesis 15:1-4

Verse 1. After these things the word of God came unto Abram in a vision, saying, Fear not, Abram: I am thy shield, and thy exceeding great reward. Verse 2. And Abram said, L<small>ORD</small> God, what wilt thou give me, seeing I go childless, and the steward of my house is this Eliezer of Damascus? Verse 3. And Abram said, Behold, to me thou hast given no seed: and, lo, one born in my house is my *heir. Verse 4. And behold, the word of God came unto him, saying, this shall not be thine heir; but he that shall come forth out of thine own bowels shall be thine heir.*

Seeing as God sees

Genesis 15: 5

Verse 5. And he brought him forth abroad, and said, "look" now toward heaven, and tell the stars, if thou be able to number them: and he said unto him, So, shall thy seed be.

God is all-knowing, and He knows what is going on in your world. He also knows the outcome of every trial. God started speaking to Abram in a vision. In that vision, He said to Abram, "Do not be afraid; I am your great reward." Abram probably asked himself what God could reward him with. He was not getting a breakthrough on who was going to head his family line.

Abram became so confused that he proposed to God the concrete plan he had already conceived in his mind. Many times, we conceive plans without even asking God for help in the first place. Abram argued that God has given me no children, therefore Eliezer, my "chief servant," will be my heir.

What a big mistake we all make! Several times, children of God act proactively without God's approval. Think for a moment! You plan on travelling without divine guidance, which is a grave mistake.

In Genesis 26: 2-3, God said to Isaac, "do not go down to Egypt, stay in the land and I will bless you. Therefore, Isaac yielded God's advice and stayed in Gerar (Genesis 26:6) where God blessed him abundantly".

It implies that Isaac had intentionally planned to leave Egypt, and God did not have His say until He told him not to leave for another place. In 1994, after completing my undergraduate programme at the Congo State University, I wanted to go to France to further my studies. I applied to several French universities but was ultimately turned down. All my efforts at applying for university admission produced nothing. I was self-centered like a man, trying to achieve things without a prompting from Heaven.

Let me say that what you have been trying to accomplish in ten years with your own strength, God can make it happen in one day.

Eliezer, the wrong choice

We tend to jeopardise our future, marriage, ministry, and destiny because we act as if God has given his seal of approval. God told Abram to "look up at the sky and count the stars." God knew that Abram's faith had to be magnified. God desires to place us in the centre of His lens for us to grasp or comprehend the magnitude of what he intends to do. When you begin to walk with God, ask him to give you the matchless binoculars that will boost your faith and cause you to be end-driven and not process-driven. Abram pointed his finger at

Eliezer, who, in the eyes of God, was not the qualified heir. God had set a marvelous end for Abram's struggle.

Beloved can I say that compromise is one of the strategies the enemy uses to deceive children of God. It can also drift someone from the Divine path and set you off God's agenda. Learn to say No when it is required. The strategy was used by Satan in the household of Abram and Sarai. The birth of Ishmael was not in God's plan but in Man's plan. Man's plan has a temporary impact whereas God's plan has eternal effect on you.

Genesis 16:1-4

> *Verse 1. Now Sarai Abram's wife bore him no children: and she had a handmaid, an Egyptian, whose name was Hagar. Verse 2. And Sarai said unto Abram, behold now, God hath restrained me from bearing: I pray thee, go in unto my maid; it may be that I may obtain children by her. And Abram hearkened to the voice of Sarai. Verse 3. And Sarai Abram's wife took Hagar her maid the Egyptian, after Abram had dwelt ten years in the land of Canaan and gave her to her husband Abram to be his wife. Verse 4. And he went in unto Hagar, and she conceived: and when she saw that she had conceived, her mistress was despised in her eyes.*

Abraham and Sara were tired of waiting on God as they grew old with no children. One day, Sarai suggested that her husband could sleep with their maidservant, Hagar. The husband welcomed the move and slept with Hagar. This couple noticed that God has not promised the birth of a child but look at Genesis 15:5 (the last section of this verse). God said, "So shall your offspring be." God told Abram that a child would be born from him. God was still in the business of fulfilling His promise. God was not late!

Let us figure out how many times we have "short-circuited the flow of God's anointing in our lives." God's anointing is like a beam of electrons moving inside an electrical wire that links heaven to earth. These electrons will enlighten your life when darkness comes your way. Let's learn to do things God's way by using and applying His word.

Please let us not compromise or find a short-cut. It will not help us at all; however, it will wear out the cord that links us to heaven, which is a source of all provisions, and eventually lead us to miss the digital print of God's touch upon your life.

Genesis 17:15-18

> *15 And God said unto Abraham, As for Sarai thy wife, thou shalt not call her name Sarai, but Sarah shall her name be. 16 And I will bless her and give thee a son also of her: yea, I will bless her, and she shall be a mother of nations; kings of people shall be of her. 17 Then Abraham fell upon his face, and laughed, and said in his heart, shall a child be born unto him that is a hundred years old? And shall Sarah that ninety years old, bear? 18 And Abraham said unto God, O that Ishmael might live before thee!*

Genesis 21:1-6

Verse 1. And God visited Sarah as he had said, and God did unto Sarah as he had spoken. Verse 2. For Sarah conceived, and bare Abraham a son in his old age, at the set time of which God had spoken to him. Verse 3. And Abraham called the name of his son that was born unto him, whom Sarah bore to him, Isaac. Verse 4. And Abraham circumcised his son Isaac being eight days old, as God had commanded him. Verse 5. And Abraham was a hundred years old, when his son Isaac was born unto him. Verse 6. And Sarah said, God hath made me to laugh, so that all that hear will laugh at me.

The birth of Isaac

God has the power to reset the old cells and make them as young as new. He (God) demonstrated that a 100-year-old man and a 90-year-old woman can have a child. What a mighty God we serve! At times, we humans see that the impossible has come, but God can still change that to "possible." Likewise, in a family setting, husband and wife should seek God's counsel before jumping on a project. Children should seek advice from their parents, just as their parents would have sought God's guidance in the same situation. Back to Isaac's story: he was the promised son, the qualified heir in Abram's line.

When we wait upon God, he beautifies our paths and makes them straight (Proverbs 3:6). It does not matter how

Chapter Six: Divine Guidance

long you have been waiting for your Isaac but keep this in mind: God will make a way where there seems to be no way. For it says in Habakkuk 2:3, "For the revelation waits for an appointed time; it speaks of the end and will not prove false." "Though it lingers, wait for it; it will certainly come and will not delay."

My first visit to Heaven in a deep sleep

One day, I had a dream. In my dream, God took me to a big city. In the city, there was light everywhere. I can't really estimate the size of that city. It seemed like I was flying from place to place instead of walking like we do here on Earth. The city had some form of structure, but I could not really delineate the streets because the roads were different from those on Earth. The roads appeared to cross over or have a convoluted pattern.

I noticed the highways, which were all very bright. As I passed somewhere, I met a person. He had the face of a human being, which was like that of a friend of mine who passed away in Malaysia in 2004. I conducted the funeral of that friend, as he was one of the leaders of the African community in Malaysia's capital city, Kuala Lumpur.

We crossed paths, and he was joyful, and we also communicated through telepathy or some other form of extrasensory perception. The message I got when we communicated, He told me, "Charles, I am here." The city was peaceful. I also saw that the late brother was much younger than he used to be before his death. I saw him in human form, but I could not describe the clothes he was wearing. After communicating with me, he walked away.

As I continued moving from place to place, I encountered a young woman. She smiled at me and greeted me. She says I am here because I was raped and killed. "After that, I came to this city," she added. When I woke up, God told me, "I took you into a very tiny portion of heaven." What I saw was just a very small fraction of heaven, which is quantitatively incomprehensible. Heaven is where we go to be with God eternally. There is peace and no more sorrow or pain in Heaven. There is not a better place to be than Heaven. I also learned that God could give anyone the grace of meeting a loved one in Heaven. Cheer up! We will surely meet some of those who left us some time ago.

My second visit to Heaven in a deep sleep

On the night of September 12, 2022, I visited Heaven in a dream. I saw myself amid trees and flowers. The environment was calm and bright, and I had a strong feeling of communicating with the plants and everything around me. That was surreal. I also saw a great number of butterflies flying above my head, and there was a sense of serenity. I asked God where I was, and he responded that I was in domain 3 of Heaven.

I also asked God where my wife was. God answered that she was in domain 5 of Heaven. The whole dream ended in awe at God talking to me in a still small voice. What I didn't get to ask God was the stratigraphy of heaven in terms of domain. I did not know what domains 3 and 5 in Heaven were. What I knew was that we—my wife and I—were in Heaven. This may sound ostentatious, but the truth is that my wife and I are saved and believe that we are heading to Heaven when our days end.

It implies that we will not live on Earth indefinitely. We will die one day and be relocated to a better place called Heaven. This second dream gave me the assurance that I must be careful with the way I live my life before I leave Earth for Heaven.

Dearly beloved in Christ, this place called Heaven is real. It is where we all are heading if we have accepted Jesus Christ as our Lord and Savior and lived a life pleasing to God.

Distinguishing God's voice from the Devil's

In this section, I will describe how God's voice sounded at the pivotal moment in my life when I accepted His call. Contrary to God's voice, the devil's voice also exists, of which we should be aware. Daily, we are exposed to both voices, which puts us in a state of confusion. It is important to learn how to discern the voice of God.

Let us examine how everything unfolded from the beginning. Before God created man, His Spirit was upon the waters. So, God spoke at the very beginning to create the whole universe (Genesis 1:1). The man and his wife first recognised God's voice in the Garden of Eden, when they sinned against God. It is evident that when God placed man in the Garden of Eden, Adam and Eve were privileged to enjoy a good relationship with God. No sin occurred in the Garden of Eden until Adam and Eve ate from the tree of the knowledge of good and evil.

They had a direct connection with their maker. So, communication with God was not a problem for them. I believe when they sinned and were chased out of the perfect confinement, they lost that perfect link with their Maker. Therefore, man lost his supernatural ability to clearly grasp God's voice when he speaks. This is the result of sin.

We grasp God's voice in a place of intimacy with him. The more we spend time with God, the more we know his voice. Let's look at the anatomy of the human body. When God created man, He gave him five sensory organs: the eyes, ears, nose, tongue, and skin. These five organs communicate with the nervous system, process information from the world outside, and react and communicate to keep the body healthy and from exposing it to dangers and diseases. I also know that some of us are born with some organic defaults that happen beyond our control. God knows why he allows such cases; everyone has natural sensory capabilities that make our lives worth living.

I know from what the Bible says that "when someone is born again, he becomes a new creation; the old has gone and the new has come." It means that there are two frequencies: the natural and the supernatural. My take here is that most people dwell in the natural frequency realm and do not use the supernatural frequency God has made available to those who choose to walk with him.

So, the new creature in Christ receives the gift from God to use the supernatural frequency that permeates our five sensory organs. This enables children of God to see and hear things differently. With this supernatural ability, children of

God can hear God speak with a different tune. They can smell something that no one could even be able to do. For instance, one day a community member came to see me for prayer. As I was praying with him, I smelled the odour of cigarettes. I asked him why he smelled of cigarettes. He smiled and said that his roommate smokes tobacco from time to time. What was relevant about the habit of smoking for his friend was to pray for him to have an encounter with Jesus, which I did. In fact, he had a good smell when he entered my house. God allowed me to change the realm while praying.

When we walk with God, He will give us the ability to tap into the higher spiritual frequencies that open when we yield to the Holy Spirit for guidance. What happens is that, at the time of our baptism in the Holy Spirit, God allows the activation mode of the supernatural frequency to turn on. Then our five senses began to function at a high frequency. Once the high frequency is activated, we need to preserve it and avoid any form of contamination (commonly related to sin) that comes from our entanglement with the world. To maintain the high frequency, we need to be prayerful each day and lovers of God's word in increasing measure.

Romans 12: 1-2

> *Verse 1. "Therefore, I urge you, brothers, and sisters, by the mercies of God, to present your bodies [dedicating all of yourselves, set apart] as a living sacrifice, holy and well-pleasing to God, which is your rational (logical, intelligent) act of worship. Verse 2. And do not be conformed to this world [any longer with its superficial values and customs] but*

be transformed and progressively changed [as you mature spiritually] by the renewing of your mind [focusing on godly values and ethical attitudes], so that you may prove [for yourselves] what the will of God is, that which is good and acceptable and perfect [in His plan and purpose for you].

It is evident that our ability to grasp God's voice is lessened when we are inclined towards worldly things; thus, God is no longer first in all we do. For example, money is good, but the love of money is the root of many vices. We cease to make room for God to mould or refine us so that we may be used by Him.

On Mount Sinai, Moses had all five of his senses fully tuned to the high frequency; that's why his skin looked different as he was shining on his descent from Mount Sinai.

When God's glory overshadows somebody

Exodus 34: 29-35

[29] When Moses came down from Mount Sinai with the two tablets of the covenant law in his hands, he was not aware that his face was radiant because he had spoken with the LORD. [30] When Aaron and all the Israelites saw Moses, his face was radiant, and they were afraid to come near him. [31] But Moses called to them; so, Aaron and all the leaders of the community came back to him, and he spoke to them. [32] Afterward all the Israelites came

Chapter Six: Divine Guidance

> *near him, and he gave them all the commands the Lord had given him on Mount Sinai.*
> *³³ When Moses finished speaking to them, he put a veil over his face. ³⁴ But whenever he entered the Lord's presence to speak with him, he removed the veil until he came out. And when he came out and told the Israelites what he had been commanded, ³⁵ they saw that his face was radiant. Then Moses would put the veil back over his face until he went in to speak with the Lord.*

When Moses came down from Mount Sinai with the two tablets of the Testimony in his hand, he did not know that the skin of his face was shining [with a unique radiance] because he had been speaking with God.

Let's pause a bit here! Moses spent quality time with God and did not even realise that his face was shining.

It appears paradoxical that there may be some visible transformation occurring within us that goes unnoticed. Have you ever been calm or still during a chaotic situation when your peers go crazy or lose control?

Moses said to the people, "Do not be afraid." Stand firm, and you will see the deliverance the LORD will bring you today. The Egyptians you see today will never return." The LORD will fight for you; you need only to be still." How come, in Exodus 14:13, someone [Moses] turned to them and boldly said, "Be still" when they thought they were going to die?

Joshua and Caleb's story

God decided to give the Promised Land to His children. But not everyone took God at His Word. God instructed Moses to send spies to the Promised Land to investigate the new land that Moses' descendants would inherit. Twelve of them went in but came back divided into two mindsets. Ten of them [the majority] reported that the land was populated with giants called Anaks. The other two [the minority], Joshua and Caleb, looked past the giants, relied on God's Word, and said we are going to possess the land. In Numbers 14:24, the Bible says, "But My servant Caleb, because he has a different spirit and has followed me fully [he has walked with me], I will bring into the land into which he entered, and his descendants shall take possession of it." I note that it can take one man to fully follow God, which could result in the outpouring of God's blessings on his descendants.

Exodus 34:30-35

> *Verse 30. When Aaron and all the Israelites saw Moses, behold, the skin of his face shone, and they were afraid to approach him. Verse 31. But Moses called to them, and Aaron and all the leaders of the congregation returned to him; and he spoke to them. Verse 32. Afterward all the Israelites approached him, and he commanded them to do everything that the Lord had said to him on Mount Sinai.*
>
> *Verse 33. When Moses had finished speaking with them, he put a veil over his face. Verse 34.*

But whenever Moses went in before the Lord to speak with Him, he would take off the veil until he came out. When he came out and he told the Israelites what he had been commanded [by God], Verse 35. The Israelites would see the face of Moses, how his skin shone [with a unique radiance]. So Moses put the veil on his face again until he went to speak with God.

God's voice can be audible

Exodus 3:4-6

⁴ When the LORD saw that he had gone over to look, God called to him from within the bush, "Moses! Moses!". And Moses said, "Here I am."
⁵ "Do not come any closer," God said. "Take off your sandals, for the place where you are standing is holy ground." ⁶ Then he said, "I am the God of your father, the God of Abraham, the God of Isaac and the God of Jacob." At this, Moses hid his face, because he was afraid to look at God.

God spoke to Moses when He noticed Moses's interest in what was going on around Him. When we hunger for the supernatural, God has no other option but to make us taste His awesomeness, holiness, and glory.

God can visit you unexpectedly

God visited Abraham and gave him a promise that at this time of the year next year, your wife will have a son (Genesis 18:1–2).

God can speak to us through the audible voice of a human being. We often think that God would speak through the appearance of an angel. But it does not always happen that way. He uses whatever means he sees fit. God spoke to the Egyptian pharaoh by passing through Moses.

In 2008, one morning, I was in my bedroom. I was immensely overwhelmed by the worries of life. I suddenly felt God's presence in the room. I heard God's voice say to me, "Charles, why are you so desperate?" Look at the wall behind you and tell me what you see. I turned around and stared at the wall. I saw an ant that was moving on the wall. God said, "Charles, I see you the same way you see this ant on the wall." "I keep an eye on your life," God added. "Do not be worried, and don't ever torture your mind with bad thoughts because you're the apple of my eye." "I will continue to care for you as I love you." I felt a strong sense of relief, as God had never spoken to me in those terms.

Fear not

Once upon a time, I went on a Christian mission trip to Singapore. During that year, not many changes were made to immigration regulations for foreigners at points of entry between Malaysia and Singapore. The law clearly stated I had to fly back into Malaysia from Singapore as I had a study

Chapter Six: Divine Guidance

permit (i.e., postgraduate student visa). Going to Singapore was my second mission trip, excluding the Christian mission trip in which I participated in the city of Dumai, Indonesia. I arrived in Singapore and worked for the ministry for a few days. On the last day of the mission trip, we began to plan for returning to Malaysia. We did not have enough money to pay for my return air ticket. I went to talk to the mission director. He thought that we should seek God's guidance and not worry too much.

The next day, early in the morning, around 6:00 a.m., I woke up, prayed, and had my breakfast. I heard God's voice tell me to go close to the fence and stand there for a while, as if I were taking some fresh air. I obeyed the voice, went out, and stood by the fence. The fence was at my chest height, and I could see cars passing by on the street in front of me. Not long after that moment, I saw a bus passing with a sticker labelled "Fear Not." The moment I read it; I knew instantly that God was up to something. Then the spirit of God reminded me of our trip back to Malaysia. God told me that you are returning to Malaysia with the team by road and that nothing bad will happen to you. I quickly went to see the mission coordinator and said to him, "God has just spoken to me to join you on this trip back to Malaysia by road, and I do not need to fly back."

The mission director said, "I believe it was God who spoke to you as you just narrated." The next morning, we set out for Kuala Lumpur, Malaysia's capital city. We arrived in Johor Bahru at the immigration entry point. We were asked to pull over and wait for the immigration officer to check all our visa statuses. Following an investigation, the officer informed us that they had made an exception for me because I was supposed to fly rather than enter Malaysia by car. Although I had a valid study visa, I should have bought an air ticket to return to Malaysia. Through that situation, God demonstrated how well he cares for us day by day.

1 Peter 3: 12

> *The Bible says, "For the eyes of the Lord are [looking favorably] upon the righteous (the upright), and His ears are attentive to their prayer (eager to answer), But the face of the Lord is against those who practice evil."*

This scripture encourages us to believe that those who behave uprightly get God's attention. He looks at them with favor.

How can we recognize God's voice?

1) We hear God's voice by improving our relationship with him. It is through a close relationship with God that we reach a level of ease in recognising God's voice.
2) We can grasp God's voice when we are less distracted. We may not know that God speaks when we are worried. It means that even if a thing is revealed to us by God, it needs to settle within us in a peaceful manner. When God prompts us to do something, we need not delay. In my own experience walking with God, God's voice always agrees with his word. Any word that contradicts God's word comes from the Devil, the prince of all lies.

God looks for someone to speak to

In Numbers 12:6, God stated. "Hear now my words: If there is a prophet among you, I, the Lord, will make myself known to him in a vision. "And I will speak to him in a dream." I believe when someone carries a prophetic grace, God will speak to him in dreams. I believe that many people have prophetic grace but do not make the most of it.

A person who is humble can easily recognise the voice of God, as the Bible says humility comes before honor. The Bible says the LORD makes the steps of the one who delights in him firm (Psalm 37:23). He guides the humble in what is right and teaches them his way. Trust in the Lord with all your heart and lean not on your own understanding; in all your ways submit to him, and he will make your paths straight (Proverbs 3:5).

Experience of automatic writing

Let me be frank up front: an exhaustive discourse on automatic writing is beyond the scope of this book. I want to highlight the most important things we need to know about automatic writing and see whether there is any biblical basis in relation to automatic writing. I first became interested in automatic writing when I started attending a religious group led by one of the religious leaders who practiced Matsouanism, a movement founded by André Matsoua in the Congo. André Matsoua was a political and social activist who fought the rise of colonialism between 1899 and 1942. Such a socio-political movement turned into a religion after the death of André Matsoua, who was highly regarded as a prophet.

So, in 1992, I became a devoted follower of the religious group. Soon after, I became involved in prayer and prophetic ministry. I used to be accurate in giving words of knowledge and wisdom to people in need during my time with the group. At some point, I was introduced to automatic writing. This type of writing, which looked like scribbling on paper, was often used during prophetic sessions. I used to read those writings and pass along the spiritual interpretation or meaning to people.

According to the literature review, automatic writing began in China in 1800. It was a long-standing Chinese practice to receive messages from deities and spirits through their mediums. In the nineteenth century, mainland China saw an increase in the number of salvationist religions (Chien-chuan, 2015). In spiritualism, it was thought that spirits held the hands of the mediums to write messages in the form of automatic writing (Kontou, 2016). Therefore, the practice was seen as a form of communication with spirits. In 2000, I became uninterested in the practice and developed an increasing disdain for automatic writing. I felt like God did not want me to continue the automatic writing as a means of staying in touch with the spirit world. God said to me to stop it, and the Holy Spirit will guide you in everything.

I want to say here that automatic writing is not needed if you are a friend of Jesus Christ. The Holy Spirit will always tell us what to say, how to say it, and when to say it. He will lead us in God's way. The words of knowledge and wisdom are gifts from God. Therefore, we should not look for other forms of spirituality to be effective in ministry or in living a life pleasing to God.

Chapter Seven
The Finish Line

I thank God for everyone who is reading this book. It is not by chance that you have become acquainted with a portion of my lived experience with God. I believe it is for our own good as God's children to be interested in what others have gone through in life so that we do not make the same mistakes or, at the very least, improve our own walk with God.

Barry (1987), in his book entitled "God and You," said that relationships develop through "mutual transparency." This author added that it is easy to say but much more difficult to practice. From his view, it implies that developing our relationship with God goes along with being open to God. God has always been open to us. But it is we who fail to engage with God in a meaningful and purposeful way.

In Isaiah 29:13, the word of God says, "And the Lord said, forasmuch as this people draw near to Me with their mouth and honour Me with their lips but remove their hearts and minds far from Me, their fear and reverence for Me are a commandment of men that is learned by repetition [without any thought as to the meaning]." According to this scripture, God is always present, but we fail to seize any opportunity to begin a relationship with God, let alone develop a lasting intimacy with him. There are three golden rules that have helped me develop an unconditional relationship with God. The three points are rejoicing, praying, and giving thanks to God in all circumstances. The three pillars of contentment are to rejoice, pray, and always give thanks to God.

Packer (1992) wrote about contentment and said, "The comprehensiveness of our contentment is another measure by which we may judge whether we really know God." It means that we know God when we are content with what we have. A child of God who complains a lot has not understood God enough. A lack of contentment may well be a foothold that the enemy might use to strike us or take us away from God. It is complaining about manna, which fragmented the relationship between the Israelites and God in the wilderness. Complaining without looking back on what God has already done for us puts us in the space of ungratefulness.

Rejoice, pray, and give thanks to God

1 Thessalonians 5:16-18

> [16] *Rejoice always,* [17] *pray continually,* [18] *give thanks in all circumstances; for this is God's will for you in Christ Jesus.*

From this scripture, it turns out that when we rejoice in all circumstances, it leads us to willingly pray to God for answers and direction and consequently immerse ourselves in thanksgiving towards God. Although we know that God is all-knowing, we can still approach him and tell him how we feel. Most times when I am down, I go to God in prayer, simply having my thoughts directed to God with a strong sense of assurance that God is going to lead me or turn around my trials. To rephrase myself, it is in a place of prayer that we realise what the will of God is in all situations. The Greek word for "will of God" is thelema. Thelema means to wish, want, choose, or purpose. In other words, God prefers that certain things happen His way rather than ours.

I have frequently encountered complicated situations for which I had no explanation until something else happened. When I was planning to get married, countless women approached me and wanted me to marry them. But many unwanted situations happened (which I will not disclose in this book—perhaps in my next publication!). I became caught up in the whirlwind of emotions, which intrinsically drained my mind to a place of being undecided or indifferent. It was not until I let God in that I began to experience clarity of mind and the strength to say no to other women and yes to my current wife (my Honey!) being my life companion. Hallelujah! All credit goes to God.

1 Chronicles 16: 34

Give thanks to the Lord, for he is good;
His love endures forever.

Here is what I have to say: The reason why we should always thank God, no matter the situation, is that the one to whom thanks are due is always good and faithful. Now, the word "good" means that He (God) does not wish you harm.

He wants the best version of you to shine in this world. This has always been my position in whatever circumstance I find myself in, thanks to God's tender mercies.

God is not just good on one occasion. He is good on all occasions. So, we cannot say, "God you have been good to me in the past, but now what is happening to me makes me question your goodness." Goodness is God's nature. Right from the beginning of creation, God has always been good. We cannot amplify God's goodness enough, nor can we question it. He is good and gives us peace.

God has filled my heart with peace on many occasions. For example, when my dad passed away, I did not have the opportunity to attend his funeral. The same thing happened when my mum passed away while I was overseas in Malaysia. When I got the bad news about the passing of my mother, my passport was at the Australian Embassy as I was waiting for my Australian entry visa to be granted. Unfortunately, I could not attend my mother's funeral. I asked God, "Why did this happen to me?" God answered me, "Charles, your thoughts are not higher than mine—that was my will." I found God's reply satisfactory.

Some spiritual nuggets

Below I have set out some scriptures that help me in my daily walk with God. Let's meditate on them every day. I found that the scriptures below have been my strength in difficult times.

2 Corinthians 5:7

The Bible says, "For we walk by faith, not by sight."

When the Bible says that we should walk by faith and not by sight, it does not mean one has to be at home and not willing to work to earn a living. If a person is physically and mentally fit, I will encourage the person to do something to earn a living. An exception is made for those who, for health reasons or retirement benefits, may choose not to work but deserve to receive some incentives or superannuation as proof of their entitlements. This scripture also means that everything works together for those who love God and are called according to His purpose. The scripture encourages that when tough times arrive, we just need to fix our eyes on God, who can turn things around for our good.

Proverbs 3:5-6.

Trust in the LORD with all your heart,
*   and do not lean on your own understanding.*
In all your ways acknowledge him,
*   and he will make straight your paths.*

We must trust God with our hearts, not our minds. The word "heart" is at least mentioned 856 times in the Bible. The word "brain" is not mentioned even once. It goes to say that we cannot use our brains to believe in what God says to us. Our mind is in the brain. It is the centre of our thoughts, and we must align our minds with God's word. God's word is a lamp to our feet and a light to our path (Psalm 119:105).

We should make the Holy Spirit our friend. We must always walk in agreement. There is an ongoing conflict between the Holy Spirit and the flesh in our daily lives. Every day, I pray to the Holy Spirit for guidance on how to proceed. He is the greatest counselor. In my geological career, I have been asking the Holy Spirit for proper guidance. I need the Holy Spirit when I write scientific articles. I always want to make sure that I don't leave the Holy Spirit out of the picture, whether in my spiritual or secular world. But it does not always work if I follow my own thinking.

One day, I misplaced my wallet in my house. I thought I lost it at the airport when disembarking the plane coming back from Melbourne, Australia. I arrived home and later needed the wallet to check a few things out. I began to look for it in my house. You know what I should have done—pray first, "God, I don't know where I misplaced my wallet; please guide me as to where it may be sitting in this house." Now, praying for the wallet's return may appear childish. But this is what we must do in all circumstances: pray when we don't even want to.

I believe we should always pray. As children of God, we must pray for even the less demanding things. That's why we say grace before eating, as we acknowledge God as the main provider. Going back to the wallet, I then decided to pause. I halted the search for a while and sat down on the couch. I relaxed a little and silently asked God, "My Lord, where could this wallet be?" I instinctively stood up and went directly to my bedroom to look under the bed. To my surprise, I found the wallet underneath my bed.

This is what the world calls the sixth sense. When we have exhausted all our options, there will be a prompting to do something that ultimately leads us to an answer. For me, the sixth sense is the supernatural ability to perceive things without conscious reasoning. So, when we are guided by the Holy Spirit, our ability to see things beyond our natural will is enhanced to a greater degree. To me, the sixth sense is a gift from God. The Holy Spirit who works in us enables us to know things that we would not know naturally.

Hebrews 12:1

> *"Therefore, since we are surrounded by so great a cloud of witnesses, let us also lay aside every weight and every sin that clings so closely, and let us run with endurance the race that is set before us."*

To close, I believe this book brought some closure to many of us who struggle in our walk with God every day. There is a race before us, and we participate in any race for a prize. Apostle Paul told the Corinthians in the biblical passage below.

1 Corinthians 9:24-27

> *24 Do you not know that in a race all the runners run, but only one gets the prize? Run in such a way as to get the prize.*
>
> *25 Everyone who competes in the games goes into strict training. They do it to get a crown that will not last, but we do it to get a crown that will last forever.*
>
> *26 Therefore I do not run like someone running aimlessly; I do not fight like a boxer beating the air.*

> *27 No, I strike a blow to my body and make it my slave so that after I have preached to others, I myself will not be disqualified for the prize.*

As we live our Christian lives, we need to focus on the finish line. One day, I participated in a 10-kilometre marathon. When we all left the departing platform, I was still strong and did not feel any pain in my feet. As the race went on, probably after 4 kilometres, I began to slow down and felt a lot of pain in my toes, and my heart was beating too fast. I saw people clapping at me to encourage me to stay in the race. I thought the clapping was not a mockery. It was a genuine gesture.

Many runners overtook me, and I kept my eyes on the finish line. I said to myself, I am not going to give up. I had to get to the arriving platform. I kept running, running, and running. When I got to the arrival place, I received so much encouragement from the race organizers. They gave me a nice white T-shirt and said, "Well done!". I was not the winner of the race, but I was among those who finished it. I strongly encourage each one of us to walk with God in a manner that brings glory to Him. The most fulfilled life on Earth is one in which God is central to every decision made without looking back.

I pray for bountiful blessings for you all, in Jesus name.

References

Anderson, N.T., Goss, S., 2009. Freedom in Christ. Monarch Books. ISBN: 978-1-85424-940-1.

Barry, W.A., 1987. God and You: Prayer as a personal relationship. Paulist Press. New York. 83p.

Brudholm, Thomas., Lang, Johannes., 2018. Emotions and Mass Atrocity: Philosophical and Theoretical Explorations. Cambridge University Press. 301p.

Bongmba, Elias K., 2007. Witchcraft and the Christian Church: Ethical Implications. In Imagining Evil: Witchcraft Beliefs and Accusations in Contemporary Africa, edited by Gerrie ter Haar, 113-142. Asmara, Eritrea: Africa World Press.

Jain, S., 2014. Earth as a Planet. In: Fundamentals of Physical Geology. Springer Geology. Springer, New Delhi. https://doi.org/10.1007/978-81-322-1539-4_4.

Kohnert, D., 1987. Magic and witchcraft: Implications for democratization and poverty-alleviating aid in Africa. Institute of African affairs, GIGA-Hamburg. https://mpra.ub.uni-muenchen.de/111475/.

Kontou, T., 2016. The Ashgate Research Companion to Nineteenth-Century Spiritualism and the Occult. Routledge. ISBN 9781317042273.

Nyabwari, B.G, and Kagema, D.N., 2014. The Impact of Magic and Witchcraft in the Social, Economic, Political and Spiritual Life of African Communities. International Journal of Humanities Social Sciences and Education 1, no. 5 (May): 9-18.

Packer, J.I., 1992. Knowing God. Hodder and Stoughton Limited. 314p.

Wang Chien-Chuan, 2015. Spirit Writing Groups in Modern China (1840–1937): Textual Production, Public Teachings, and Charity. In Modern Chinese Religion II 1850–2015, edited by Vincent Goossaert, Jan Kiely and John Lagerwey, Leiden: Brill, vol. 2, 651–684.

Chabra, S., Rai, D., Balachandra, A.S., Joseph Shibu., Meghashree V., 2014. "The Emotional and Psychological Aspects of Hate and Enmity". Journal of Evolution of Medical and Dental Sciences 2014; Vol. 3, Issue 49, October 02; Page: 11715-11725, DOI: 10.14260/jemds/2014/3539.

Southwick, S.M., Bonanno G.A., Masten, A.S., Panter-Brick, C., Yehuda R., 2014. Resilience definitions, theory, and challenges: interdisciplinary perspectives. Eur J Psychotraumatol. 2014 Oct 1; 5. doi: 10.3402/ejpt.v5.25338. PMID: 25317257; PMCID: PMC4185134.

Endorsement 1

In the summary, Charles makes the point that the purpose of the book is to instill hope that regardless of the situations or seasons that we may be enduring that God is still in control. That statement is a beautiful summation of a book that encapsulates the obvious intellect that Charles poses alongside his unwavering faith in God. Charles has the ability to take the reader to moments of his life that make you feel like you are sitting at the kitchen table eating porridge made from cassava roots or walking his father to the shops for groceries.

I highly recommend this book, and well-done Charles.

Shaun White, Senior Pastor
C3 Church, Hobart, Australia

Endorsement 2

In this book *Deep Times with God*, the author challenges us to live in close contact with God and to have hope even when everything around us is falling apart. In fact, we frequently encounter these wonderful moments of contact with God when He promptly answers our prayers and grants our wants. But the moment we experience hardships in our lives, this connection with God is broken. Consequently, we are no longer aware of the living presence of God in our lives. We now feel a great distance from God who was once so close to us.

In our homes, in our heart of hearts, we are tempted by murmurings like the children of Israel of old in their tents (Psalm 106: 24-25). We rebel against God, even to the point of occasionally creating golden calf statues for us to grovel before and worship. (Exodus 32: 1 – 14)

Today, the world provides us a lot of false hope and forces us to do a lot of things that go against God's desire. Just like false doctrines that make us dangle, through false servants of God, a Christian life in which the cross no longer exists. While the Lord invites us to take up our cross to follow him (Matthew 10: 38 and Luke 9: 23).

The cross is central to the Christian walk. This cross implies a trusting faith, which hopes, which never doubts whatever the circumstances. The mountains can shake, the waves of the sea can rise: this faith remains intact.

We can spend a whole night fishing empty-handed: this faith trusts that the Lord is waiting for us on the shore with fish cooked on the coals to restore our strength and come to fill our human insufficiency by giving us a miraculous fishing experience.

Glory be to our God for what He has put in our midst, brothers, and sisters in Christ who, in all circumstances, always keep a trusting faith, which never wavers despite tribulations.

Our beloved Dr. Charles MAKOUNDI is one of those people who always look to the Master, the Lamb of God immolated on the Cross.

From the trials he went through in his life, he knew how to count on the Love, fidelity and unfailing promises of the Most-High God who revealed himself to him as being the ALMIGHTY; just as He had done with Abram (Genesis 17:1).

These trials therefore strengthened his faith and then helped him, in his Christian walk, to harmoniously reconcile his family LIFE, his professional LIFE and his RESPONSIBILITIES of the ministry.

I cannot auscultate the role of his wife, my dear youngest sister, Claire Michelle MAKOUNDI, who has always been by his side like:

- An essential support, always, in the good as well as the darkest days, without ever making reproaches especially when the times were difficult.

- An attentive ear who knows how to listen, analyze to weigh up and give her opinion.

- A shoulder to lean on in moments of depression to regain strength.

It is a privilege for us, their loved ones, to see the trajectory of their lives, where they have gone and how God has supported them to overcome all the trials encountered in their journey: from the Congo to Malaysia and then in Tasmania today.

I will conclude by saying that to have the blessings, you must be in the presence of the One who blesses: therefore, spend deep moments with him; otherwise, live a life of true fellowship with God (Revelation 3:20).

Paul MAKAMBILA, New Caledonia.

ENDORSEMENT 3

It is a great honor and privilege to recommend *Deep Times with God*, written by a Man who fears God and loves the Holy Spirit, a true son of God, Dr. Charles Makoundi, whom I personally know with his loving wife Michelle Makoundi for 22 years!

This book traces a lifetime, the origins of this man who had great experiences with this great God, and which had as results: the impact of a lifetime, his restricted entourage and several people who will be encouraged in their personal walk with Jesus Christ!

Deep Times with God not only talks about what a man could see, live with God, but also that the Eternal God can take an ordinary person and do extraordinary things with him, and ultimately make him a vessel of honor!

This book is truly captivating, easy to read to understand the mysteries of the depth of true intimacy with The Creator, Jesus Christ, and the Holy Spirit!

John 14:1 "Do not let your heart be troubled. Believe in God and believe in me".

John 14:13 "And whatever you ask in my name, I will do, that the Father may be glorified through the Son".

Happy Reading to All!

Ange-Marie Mukieya Malila
Pastor of Restoration Centre, Belgium
Founder of Watch & Pray
Daughter in the Lord of Dr. Charles Makoundi

Endorsement 4

Without a deep understanding of the things of God and the ways through which God works in our lives to bring about his plans and purposes for our lives, it is in fact impossible to grow and reach full spiritual maturity and potential in one's life and walk with the Lord. Deep Times with God is a unique book in that Rev. Dr. Charles Makoundi leans unselfishly on his personal experiences, some of which are deep-buried childhood memories, to map out how God used those seemingly hard, at times earth-shattering, life-altering adverse situations to shape, mold, and guide the person that he will become, working all things together for Charles's good and His glory (Rom 8:28).

God only takes us through deep times to bring about his bigger, better, and deeper plans for our lives to bring the best out of us. Many writers have shared and spoken on their relationship with God; Charles has however taken this one step further by bringing us along and taking us on a voyage in the peculiar universe of his lifelong experiences from central Africa and South-east Asia to his current residence in Australia.

This book gives you precious nuggets and concludes with the three pillars of contentment to which God calls every one of His children: rejoicing always, praying, and thanking God in all circumstances. Though we are troubled on every side, yet not distressed; we are perplexed, but not in despair; persecuted, but not forsaken; cast down, but not destroyed (2 Cor 4:8–9), because we choose to rejoice in the Lord in the face of adversity. When deep has called upon deep and real trust has developed with God, we cease to worry, and Phil 4:6 becomes real in our lives: "in everything, by prayer and supplication with thanksgiving, let your requests be made known to God".

A life that is impacted by God is one that is full of thanksgiving. Paul said in his writing to the churches at Philippi and Thessaloniki that he thanked God always for their remembrance and prayed for them with joy. Thanksgiving sets us on course to experience God's best and His everlasting peace. This book will challenge you to dive deep into God to find meaning and see His hand in the very circumstances that are surrounding your life right now!

Alain R. Mizelle
Pastor, teacher & Entrepreneur
Ambassadors Christian Centre
Montreal, Canada

Endorsement 5

"Deep Times with God" is a compelling read with the author exposing his vulnerabilities by sharing from his personal walk with Jesus Christ to whom he gives all the glory. This authenticity reaches out to any reader who may be feeling lost, questioning the purpose of their life, or struggling with issues.

Personal lived accounts as presented to us by author Dr Charles Makoundi are both engaging and convincing of the need for, and blessing of, a life walked in lock step with Christ.

As a highly qualified scientist Charles Makoundi has an enquiring mind yet he has the humility and understanding to acknowledge that science without God loses its essence. Same with the human walk. As Makoundi quotes, Jeremiah 29:11 "I know the plans I have for you, says the Lord, plans for peace and not for woe, to give you a future and hope." This eternal promise remains as true today as when first uttered by the prophet Jeremiah thousands of years ago.

The reliance on Biblical texts assures the reader that this comforting book is soundly based on God's Word and not on temporary feel-good platitudes.

This home spun, easy to read book is a handy resource for the caring person to have on stand-by ready to provide to that friend or acquaintance in need of practical guidance, reassurance or motivation in their faith walk. Revealing the trials of being tested and our natural human reaction to respond negatively is rebuked with the experience of lived knowledge that trials provide us with the best outcomes for our own growth and assurance they have a Divine purpose.

Dr Makoundi reminds us we need to stay focused on the Saviour and His Word as revealed in the Bible as the path to a fulfilled life. So fulfilled a life that the author confidently proclaims that he has no fear of death because he knows he will be welcomed by his Heavenly Father.

Lovingly dedicated to his extended family and the Glory of God 'Deep Times with God' is a Biblically based readable book suitable for any reader interested in deepening their faith or those out searching or needing of reassurance. Every reader will benefit from the wisdom and truths that appear on every page.

Eric Abetz - Former Government Senate Leader
Tasmania, Australia

About the Author

Rev. Dr. Charles Makoundi holds a doctorate degree in economic geology from the University of Tasmania, Australia. As a community leader, he is the national leader of the Australian Congolese Association (Bana Congo Brazza), the chairman of the Tasmanian African Community Forum (TAFRIC), and an advisor to the African Communities Council of Tasmania (ACCT). He also serves as Treasurer of the Culturally Diverse Alliance of Tasmania (CDAT).

He works for the Department of State Growth, Mineral Resources Tasmania, as a Geoscience Data Officer. He currently holds a University Associate position at the University of Tasmania and contributes to geoscience education and research. He has published several scientific articles in peer-reviewed, high-impact journals. He has been a reviewer and editor for several international journals. He holds a certificate in ministry training from the School of Acts, Malaysia, and a diploma in cross-cultural ministry from the Malaysian Centre for Global Ministry. After being baptized by water immersion in 1994, he became involved in prayer ministry and pastoral work in his local Congolese church before going to Malaysia as a missionary.

He and his wife contributed to church planting in Malaysia and were the lead pastors of Oikos International Fellowship between 2005 and 2007 in Kuala Lumpur, Malaysia. In 2008, they founded Jesus Power Ministry International in Malaysia before moving to Australia. Rev. Dr. Charles Makoundi was ordained as a minister of the gospel of Jesus Christ by the Ambassadors of Christ Ministry.

www.ingramcontent.com/pod-product-compliance
Lightning Source LLC
LaVergne TN
LVHW051125080426
835510LV00018B/2244